The Art and Science of Self-Discovery: Explore your Personality, Discover Your Strengths, Gain Self-Awareness, and Design a Life That Fits You

By Peter Hollins,
Author and Researcher at petehollins.com

Table of Contents

The Art and Science of Self-Discovery: 3

Table of Contents 5

Introduction 7

Chapter 1. The Origins of Identity and Personality 13

Chapter 2. The Big Five Personality Traits 33

Chapter 3. Myers, Briggs, and Keirsey 61

Chapter 4. Unconscious Upbringings 85

Chapter 5. Nurture Over Nature? 107

Chapter 6. The Stories We Create 125

Chapter 7. Self-Awareness Questions 1

Chapter 8. Effecting Change 1

Chapter 9. Personality Potpourri 1

Summary Guide 1

Introduction

The first time I went to New York, I was a young child and incredibly excited. I spent the bulk of my childhood in a small town with fewer than 10,000 residents, so you can imagine how thrilling the prospect of unending skyscrapers and Times Square was to me.

It didn't disappoint, and I was able to check a multitude of touristy events off my bucket list—going to the top of the Empire State Building, sailing out to the Statue of Liberty, riding a subway, and, yes, visiting Times Square.

I have to say, everything lived up to what I had built it up to be in my head—except riding the subway. Where I expected a futuristic mode of transport, I was in reality sitting among graffiti that was far too explicit for a child my age to see. And then there were the people on the subway.

By that, I mean normal New Yorkers, not homeless people or vagrants. This is where my background becomes important. In a small town, you likely know almost everyone you are going to run into, or at least someone in their family. In some sense, you lose all anonymity, and you are essentially held accountable for every moment you are in public—because you are being watched by someone who knows you. This does enforce a certain type of hospitality and small-town charm—everyone smiles to each other and tries to help out whenever possible. Whatever the reason, it creates a nice atmosphere for everyone.

But this was not so in New York. If you're from New York, you are probably nodding your head at this while simultaneously shaking your head at my small-town naiveté. New Yorkers, I later discovered, have quite a reputation for being dismissive (at best) to strangers and while in public. Perhaps it was because everyone was so busy and was rushing off to urgent business, but you don't tend to see that type of behavior in other large cities. So what caused this culture of directness and terseness?

If you took a pair of twins and put one of them in my small town and the other in New York to grow up, would the New Yorker instinctually bark at people walking slowly on the sidewalk? Would they have the same temperament through the miracle of biology, or would their environments completely take over that role?

It's a question that we still can't really answer. What causes people to be the way they are? Is it a reflection of their biological imperative that they can't escape, or is it a product of observing what's around them and emulating what they see? For me, when I moved to Seattle later in life, I suddenly began to understand the frustration people felt in big cities. I may not bark at people on a daily basis, but I've done it internally to an extent I never knew could exist.

This is just one piece of the puzzle when it comes to the art and science of self-discovery. Why do we turn out the way we do, and what role do we have in that, if any?

But it's not just a question that we should answer out of luxury or in our spare time. It's a question that can shape our very lives. If you don't know what influenced you in the past or what type of personality and identity you currently possess, then it's almost an inevitability that the decisions you make for yourself are going to be suboptimal or just plain bad.

Self-knowledge is what allows us to reach happiness and fulfillment—because we know what makes us happy and fulfilled. Does it serve an introvert well to have a job where she is forced to small talk with clients and customers for hours a day? Or might it be more beneficial to her sanity to find a job where facetime with people is severely limited?

It seems trivial, but these things accumulate over time. At some point in the future, you can either look back at your life and feel good about it or feel that you were living someone else's. The latter option is a frightening thought, so it's time to start your journey to self-discovery so you can design a life that fits just right.

Chapter 1. The Origins of Identity and Personality

People have unique personalities. What an understatement.

On the road, some people handle their frustration with other drivers differently than others. Getting cut off can trigger one person's rage and cause them to lash out with loud expletives to themselves and others. Others might simply brush it off and move on to their destination, not even remembering that it happened an hour later. What causes this massive difference?

A living being, regardless of species, possesses a specific personality and identity that is unique to his/her own.

Biologically speaking, people have been known to inherit particular personality types from their parents, no matter how hard they try to avoid it. There are also theories that state personalities are a result of one's environment. Can there really be one definitive answer as to how we turn into the people that we do?

Just exactly where do our personalities come from? Are they learned or innately part of one's destiny? Can we find an answer to what has been an ongoing debate and the subject of study by psychologists, scientists, and philosophers for decades?

This chapter aims to explore the history, origins, and modern biology of personality and how people can understand themselves better. It works to integrate different theories and studies that have attempted to prove why humans are the way they are.

Humorism

To understand how we arrived at the modern take on personality, it's necessary to start from a historical perspective. It comes as no surprise that many theories stem from philosophers in ancient Greek eras.

The Greeks first theorized that one could classify types of personalities through "humors," then moved onto specific types of temperaments that formed thereof. This was called *humorism*.

It was Hippocrates (460–370 BC) who first developed and defined it as a medical theory. He believed that a person's mood and emotions came from an excess of four specific bodily fluids: yellow bile, black bile, blood, and phlegm. Thus, in varying amounts, these represented a person's personality traits and general temperaments. In Galen's (129–c.200 AD) dissertation *De Temperamentis*, he studied and developed the typology of these temperaments. He was determined to find the physiological reasons behind people's behaviors.

Derived from the four elements of air, earth, wind, and fire, Galen classified these behaviors as being either hot or cold and dry or wet components. A balance between the qualities was also something that could be possible and what Galen worked to prove as being the ideal personality. Galen theorized that an ideal personality comprised of a complementary balance of hot or cold and dry or wet.

However, realizing that such balance was unlikely to characterize most people in society, he eventually codified four temperaments: choleric, melancholic, sanguine, and phlegmatic. These were respectively named after the bodily humors that Hippocrates noted. When humors would excessively produce, this would create an imbalance in paired qualities.

Yellow Bile: Choleric Temperament
This temperament is also known as the "leader" type, where a person is characterized as being confident, ambitious, overbearing, and passionate. This strong-

willed personality tends to be more extroverted than introverted.

Black Bile: Melancholic Temperament
The more calming characteristic of the humors, melancholics tend to be reserved and thoughtful. They can be moody and expect a high level of perfectionism. They also value alone time and are mindful of making decisions.

Blood: Sanguine Temperament
No social event can be without the social butterflies. Sanguine temperaments are people-oriented and are deemed to be the "happy-go-lucky" types. But they can be a bit frazzled and disorganized.

Phlegm: Phlegmatic Temperament
Loyalty and consistency are the best terms to describe phlegmatic types. They are quiet and stable, which are what other people appreciate to keep their relationships more balanced. They can also be seen as submissive due to their overly trustworthy behaviors.

Many people will identify with some, if not all, of these humors. There may be particular days or situations that cause people to portray one or more of these temperaments at any given time. But generally speaking, one type of humor will be more dominant over the others on a consistent basis.

Overall, *humorism* greatly centers around the individual and unique compositions. It was one of the original approaches to the study of personality and what made even a pair of twins different and distinct.

Structural Model

Although *humorism* made sense to most, it still didn't explain the *reasons* behind an individual's personality. Different humors may have aggregated in different amounts in people, but what caused it? Was it just a birthright or curse?

Famous Austrian neurologist and psychologist Sigmund Freud (1856–1939) had his own way of describing someone's personality. Perhaps the best-known model of personality, though somewhat dubious in real-life effectiveness and application, is known as the *structural model of personality*. You know it as the three components of the *id, ego, and superego*.

Freud believed that a person's psyche was centrally controlled by these unconscious three components. He also believed that each component had a direct influence over the other, thus shaping someone's personality. Just like humorism, if there was any imbalance between the three components, it would give rise to certain types of personalities (and also personality disorders).

Id: "Just give it to me; I want it now."
The id follows the pleasure principle. Basically, a person will behave in a manner to reap a reward in the end. The id is the primitive and instinctive component of all three. As such, it functions solely on fulfilling those primal drives, such as hunger, sex, and all forms of pleasure. It is a single-minded drive.

An infant is the perfect representation of the id because an infant only knows what it wants and cries when it is not received. Infants are impulsive and lack the ability to empathize or control themselves. It's only later that a newborn can actually develop an ego and superego through learned situations. The infant wanting dessert has no regard for reality. Instead, he is wishful in his thinking and wants that dessert if it's the last thing he'll ever get. This is where ego comes into play.

Ego: "I really want that, but how can I realistically get it?"
The id can't last forever in the real world in conjunction with other people and their own needs.

The ego eventually takes over the id as the principle of reality. It helps a person acknowledge that there are limitations and external factors to someone's behavior. The same child will learn that he may not always get a dessert, especially if he acts up and throws his food around the kitchen. These were factors that weren't ever present before and he's able to acknowledge now.

Think of the ego as being the mediator between the struggles of unrealistic id and reality. Basically, this is where a child learns to make decisions while actually weighing consequences and things other than bare desire. Reasoning is one characteristic of the ego as opposed to the more irrational id. The ego works by strategizing realistic ways to meet the demands of the id.

This process usually means that there must be a compromise at some point. Sometimes, it's necessary to postpone rewards so that one won't feel the negative consequences when reacting irrationally. The ego is more aware of social norms and decencies, thus teaching a person how to compose himself/herself in situations. There's no right or wrong. The goal of the ego is to attain reward without harm. In a power struggle, the ego will always fall to the id. But then there's the superego.

Superego: "I want that, but not if it makes me a terrible person."

The superego helps the individual identify values and morals set by society and forces him or her to be more self-aware. Basically, the superego is conscience sitting on your shoulder asking whether you should do something or not.

The superego can also be seen to suppress the primal urges of the id, but in a different way from the ego. Remember, the ego suppresses the id by reminding it of the practical realities of the world, while the superego suppresses the id by giving a test of values and morals before acting.

Id, Ego, and Superego—How it All Plays Out
An infant initially believed that he could finish his meal and then a dessert would always come after (his id). However, he didn't account for other factors while he ate his dinner. If he threw his food around and made a mess, he learned that this was deemed as a negative behavior that could alter his happy ending (his ego). Finally, he felt shameful about disrespecting his parents and learned to correct his behavior in the future (his superego).

Overall, Freud concluded that the three components of the psyche all had their own interests at play. This is what caused a person to think and act in a particular way. The child first acted out of selfishness and eventually learned to channel his emotions not only in favor of himself, but also to meet social norms.

Many psychologists and psychoanalysts were greatly influenced by the works and studies of Freud. But the fact that it relies completely on the unconscious drives makes it nearly impossible to prove and quantify. It becomes too inconsistent, and there was no hard data to back it up.

Plus, it has also been noted that Freud's theory doesn't account for unpredicted natures of human behavior and free will. But his theory is one that is interesting and can be used to help people understand their traits and motivation for behavior.

The Biological Basis of Personality

Although theories have studies to help support their claims, biology is certainly more compelling in delivering concrete answers. Many theories get challenged as a result of lack of data or research. So there is a more modern look into personality and what can be understood about the brain.

First, biology tells researchers that personalities are a result of natural selection. For humans in general, the traits that people have now were more vital to their ancestors. The well-known principle of "survival of the fittest" is considered to have created at least the baseline for our modern personalities.

Over time, people began to develop characteristics that are split into two categories: intrasexual selection traits and intersexual selection traits.

Intrasexual selection is what happens when two people of the opposite sex are attracted to one another. In a relationship, two people begin to exhibit particular personality traits that keep the other interested and engaged.

Over time, these became instinctual mating behaviors that inform our personalities.

Intersexual selection occurs when characteristics aspire to intimidate and defeat rivals of the same sex—in other words, competition. People may describe this as competing for the same job or even a parking spot at the grocery store. Having a competitive edge makes one feel empowered and motivated to do well over an opponent. Over time, these defensive and offensive competitive drives also became instinctual. It is highly likely that these evolved traits were hardwired with different brain structures as a result of these intra- and intersexual means.

More contemporary-thinking psychologists and scientists found that there is a direct correlation between the sizes of various brain parts and the different traits in personality. In fact, the sizes of various brain parts were what they chose to focus on primarily, and their studies revealed some interesting and notable findings.

At the University of Minnesota, a study asked 116 subjects to answer a series of questions pertaining to personality. Then the subjects were also given a brain imaging test where specific regions of their brains were photographed and studied.

The data sort consisted of categorizing the study participants into five different factors for personality traits, the Big Five, which will be covered in greater detail later in this book:

- conscientiousness
- agreeableness
- extraversion
- openness
- neuroticism

The following data was compiled and disseminated for a conclusion:

1. Researchers were able to discover that extroverted people tend to have a bigger medial orbitofrontal cortex. This is located right above and behind the eyes.

2. People considered to be more conscientious had larger lateral prefrontal cortexes.
3. Neurotically driven individuals had bigger brain regions such as the cortices, which meant this was responsible for their negative emotions.
4. Agreeable people also had larger cortical regions. However, as opposed to neurotic people, these regions are a little more wrinkled and folded. This meant they are able to empathize with others and their thoughts.
5. It is still unclear as to how brain regions correspond with openness and intellect.

The results speak for themselves. There is a very real biological basis for differences in personality. Nature versus nurture is always a compelling debate, and this signifies that they will always be inseparable.

Studies such as these have opened up more perspectives and doors to the understanding of the brain and personalities. Researchers and scientists can use this data and these findings to bridge the learning gap of personality traits. It isn't necessarily a one-all-be-all approach, but rather a foundation toward more definitive answers to a longstanding debate. How it happens is a subject for another debate.

They could now directly relate a person's brain graph to how this person behaves. This type of research can also be used to predict a person's behavior and personality traits.

Why Does This Matter?

Learning about one's personality and identity is essential to living the most optimal and conscientious life. Self-awareness and knowing where specific traits come from are the foundations for understanding oneself. In a world where people are constantly trying to find themselves and their purpose for living, it seems pretty clear that they can start with studying their own personal character traits.

Lacking an understanding of personality and identity will mean that no one knows why they may act in certain ways. They may not understand how they got to where they are.

They may not see the successes of overcoming obstacles that helped them rise above. Most importantly, they would not be able to decipher their own needs and wants in any situation.

Take a simple day-to-day activity of exercise. If a man knows that he is more of an introvert, he may opt to take hikes on trails or utilize headphones at the gym to keep to himself. He will spend a lot of time avoiding people and he is well aware of that. For an extrovert, he might rather take a cycling class or work out with a few friends. He'll do anything to be the social person he knows he is.

Both individuals know what they prefer as a result of understanding their own personalities. Thus, they both place themselves in situations they know they can tackle. Had the introvert not known what pushed him over the edge, he could have had an anxiety attack when walking into high-energy aerobics class. Or had the extrovert strolled into a yoga class, he would have been bored out of his mind.

When choosing a career path, people should have a confident understanding of who they are in order to take the right path. If someone is great at design and creation, she may not pursue a career in accounting. A prospective engineer wouldn't work toward becoming a chef. Knowing themselves allows them to pursue their own strengths and hide their weaknesses.

Having a sense of self-awareness allows one to make more mindful decisions and take meaningful paths that are specific to one's own needs. The more that someone is well-acquainted with himself or herself, the easier it is to exhibit real and appropriate character traits. He or she can capitalize on this knowledge and follow a driven, relevant lifestyle. It is then that the search for identity and purpose is at the center of his or her control.

Takeaways:

- The study of personality and identity has been a compelling issue for as long as we have been sentient beings. Like many disciplines, study seemed to have begun in ancient Greece with the theory of humorism—where four separate bodily fluids were present in the body in varying quantities that gave rise to different personalities and four temperaments in particular.

- One of the most seminal personality theories was put forth by Sigmund Freud hundreds of years later. This is known as the structural model, and you know it by its three components: the id, ego, and superego. Like the humors, they worked together in varying amounts to form a unique personality. The id is a hedonist, the ego is the mediator, while the superego is the conscience.
- There is a strong biological basis for differences in personality. First, intrasexual and intersexual traits have formed the baseline for our modern personalities in many ways. Second, there are literal biological and physical differences between those who score differently on the Big Five personality traits.

- Why does this all matter? It's simple, actually. If you don't know where you are coming from and where you are right now, how are you supposed to know where you should go next?

Chapter 2. The Big Five Personality Traits

Chances are, at some point in your life, you've taken a personality, career aptitude, or relationship test to learn more about yourself. The quest to find out what makes human beings happier is as universal as the desire to understand why. What makes some people behave, think, and feel certain ways and not others? Why do humans engage in habitual patterns, even when those could be to their detriment?

The answer may lie in the Big Five personality traits, a theory that dissects the human psyche into five broad characteristics. These five simple factors could determine the very complex question you've been chasing: what makes you *you*?

It's a theory that dates back to 1949, in research published by D.W. Fiske. Since then, it's been gaining popularity and has been written about by the likes of Norman (1967), Smith (1967), Goldberg (1981), and McCrae and Costa (1987).

Instead of evaluating you as a whole, this is one of the first personality theories to break you down into five traits: openness to experience, conscientiousness, extroversion, agreeableness, and neuroticism.

You may have heard of these before. Terms like introvert and extrovert are thrown around a lot these days, but what do they really mean? They're two ends of the spectrum. Each trait has two extremes, and although we may not want to admit it, every one of us embodies all of these five traits to some degree.

According to this theory, it's how much of each and where we land in the range between the extremes that determine our unique personality. Let's break it down.

Openness to Experience

The first of the Big Five personality traits determines how willing you are to take risks or try something new. Would you ever jump out of a plane? How about pack up and move halfway around the world to immerse yourself in a new culture? If your answer to both of those questions was a resounding yes, then you probably score high in your openness to experience. That is, you seek out the unknown.

At one extreme, people who are high in openness are curious and imaginative. They go in search of new adventures and experiences. They can get bored easily and turn to their creativity to uncover new interests and even daring activities. These people are flexible and seek out variety in their daily life. For them, routine is not an option.

At the other end of the spectrum, people who are low on the openness scale prefer continuity and stability to change. They are practical, sensible, and more conventional than their peers. Change is not their friend.

In the real world, most people fall somewhere in between these opposites, but where you find yourself on the spectrum could reveal a lot about who you are and what you excel at.

Do you dream of being a CEO or at the head of your field, for instance? Openness has been linked to leadership. If you're able to entertain new ideas, think outside the box, and adapt quickly to new situations, you're more likely to become and succeed as a leader (Lebowitz, 2016).

It was Apple cofounder Steve Jobs's decision to audit a calligraphy class in 1973 that would lead to the groundbreaking typography in Mac computers years later. At the time, no one associated computers with beautiful fonts, but Jobs saw something that no one else could. He embraced the calligraphy class, sought to change the way people thought about computers, and opened himself up to a new vision of the future.

People who are open also tend to embrace universalism, seeing values as equally applicable to all people (Douglas, Bore & Munro, 2016). They choose peace and tolerance over conflict and discrimination. They see all people as similarly deserving of justice and equality. And they may pursue careers that lead them to fight for their ideals.

A quick look back over your life may reveal just how open to experience you are and how much of this trait you possess.

Conscientiousness

Idealism, creativity, and thirst for new experiences can take you far in life, but how hard you're willing to work for your goals is another determinant of your success. That's where the second Big Five comes in: conscientiousness. This is the personality trait that makes you careful and cautious. You're vigilant in your actions and often think twice, or three times, before making a decision, especially if it wasn't in your original plans.

People who have high levels of conscientiousness tend to be extremely focused on their goals. They plan things out, focusing on the detailed tasks at hand, and they stick to their schedules. They have better control over their impulses, emotions, and behaviors, such that they are able to focus more of their energy on their professional success. While they may not live as adventurously as their peers, they do tend to live longer, thanks in part to their healthier habits.

At the other end of the spectrum, people who are not so conscientious tend to be more impulsive and disorganized. They become demotivated by too much structure, can procrastinate on important work, and have a weaker ability to control their behavior. This can lead to more self-destructive habits, such as smoking and substance abuse, and an overall inability to get things done. Impulse control is no easy feat for them.

So how conscientious are you? Do you like schedules at work but still find yourself avoiding exercise when you get home? You may embrace some aspects of conscientiousness, like schedules and to-do lists, and not others, like exercising or performing other healthy habits. Most people land somewhere in the middle of the conscientiousness spectrum, but if you can find ways to embrace planning and order a little bit more, you could be setting yourself up for success.

Conscientiousness has been linked to better success after training (Woods, Patterson, Koczwara & Sofat, 2016), more effective job performance (Barrick & Mount, 1991), higher job satisfaction, and careers with greater prestige and higher incomes (Judge, Higgins, Thoresen & Barrick, 1999). A study by Soldz and Vaillant (1999) also found that high levels of conscientiousness have helped people better adjust to the challenges of life that will inevitably sneak up on you.

Say, just as you're leaving the office for the day, a colleague comes with another task that he needs urgently. How would you react? If you decide to stay a few more minutes, complete the task, and take your delay in stride, you likely rank higher on the conscientious scale. But if you are already overwhelmed with work as it is and don't see how you can get it done, you may fall toward the other extreme.

Conscientiousness is the preventative medicine we could all use to stop problems before they start.

<u>Extroversion</u>

When problems do arise, enthusiasm and optimism are two characteristics that can help carry you through, and that's where extroversion comes in—the third of the Big Five traits. This is the trait that defines how outgoing or social you are.

Extroverts are easy to spot. They're the life of the party, they've got lots of energy, and they know how to talk. Extroverts draw their energy from being around other people and thrive on being the center of attention. For that reason, they maintain a wide circle of friends and take every opportunity to meet new people.

At the other extreme are people who often find extroverts exhausting to be around: introverts. Why spend time trying to make conversation with large groups of people when you can be at home with your own thoughts? Introverts aren't shy; they simply prefer solitude to socializing or calm to chaos.

Do you wish office parties would never end, or do you feel drained after about an hour? Do you enjoy meeting new people, or would you prefer to be cuddled up at home with a good book? Are you a morning person, or do you truly wake up when the sun goes down?

If you're often the last one to leave a social gathering, you enjoy being around people, and you thrive on the late-night hours, you likely rank high on the extroversion scale. If, on the other hand, you dread the thought of going to parties, would rather stay home alone, and prefer to wake up bright and early to start your day, you're probably more of an introvert.

Depending on the day, you may be inclined to go either way. However, by and large, people typically place somewhere along the spectrum between the two. And while it might have once been thought that those who wake up early and keep to themselves were prone to be more successful, extroversion is actually a strong predictor of who will be a leader (Barrick & Mount, 1991).

Think about it: if you're comfortable being around people, they're more likely to be comfortable around you. If you like starting conversations, you could find yourself with a wider social network in which to mobilize. And if you're more assertive, people might be more prone to believe in you. These are all the makings of a successful leader.

That's not to say that introverts can't lead. It may just require taking a few more steps outside of their comfort zone.

Agreeableness

When you're stepping out of your comfort zone, it never hurts to have a helping hand or someone to encourage you along the way. These kinds of people rank high on the agreeableness scale—the fourth of the Big Five personality traits. This is the trait that identifies how kind and sympathetic you are and how warm and cooperative you are with others.

Do you tend to take a big interest in other people and their problems? When you see others going through difficulties, does it affect you, too? If you're empathetic and caring toward others and driven by the desire to help, you may be quite an agreeable person. You feel their pain and are driven to do something about it.

At the other of the spectrum, people who are less agreeable may find they take less of an interest in other people's lives. Instead of trying to work together to solve a problem, they may be more content to go it alone. Because of their nature, they may often be perceived as offensive or unpleasant to be around.

We all have different thresholds for how much we're willing to do for others and how much we're willing to work together. That limit is where you rank on the agreeableness spectrum.

Why people are so agreeable is still up for debate. For some, it's the genuine concern for the well-being of others. For others, it's the result of social pressure and accepted norms. Fear of consequences can be a motivating factor. Some agreeable people may be acting that because they are petrified of social confrontation. Whatever the case, research has shown that agreeable people are rarely cruel, ruthless, or selfish (Roccas, Sagiv, Schwartz & Knafo, 2002).

If you're looking for ways to be a little bit happier, figuring out where you lie on the agreeable index may be a good way to start.

Neuroticism

We all have those days when nothing is how it seems. You think your coworkers are out to get you. You're so anxious you can't sleep. You feel like you're caught in a Woody Allen film. But if you find yourself having lots of those days, to the point where you feel more down than you do up, you may have high levels of the last of the Big Five traits: neuroticism. This is the personality trait that essentially measures how emotionally stable you are. It identifies your ability to remain steady and balanced versus anxious, insecure, or depressed.

Neurotics tend to approach life with a high dose of anxiety. They worry more than most and their moods can shift quickly and with little prompting. This kind of behavior can make them prone to being stressed or even depressed.

Those on the less neurotic side of the spectrum tend to be more emotionally stable. When stress comes their way, they have an easier time dealing with it. Bouts of sadness are few and far between, and they see fewer reasons to stress about whatever may come their way.

Do you find yourself using humor to cope with a challenge, or do problems tend to stress you out? Are you pretty levelheaded all day long, or do you switch from hot to cold in a heartbeat? If you take things in stride and usually only have one mood per day, you're probably less neurotic than others. But if you have many moods in the space of a short amount of time and are anxious more often than not, you're probably on the more neurotic side.

We all fall somewhere along this spectrum, but how you answer these questions is a good indication of which way you lean.

If you're higher on the neurotic scale, you're more likely to suffer from poor job performance, and it may take more to get you motivated (Judge & Ilies, 2002). Setting goals for yourself and sticking to them could be a challenge.

However, being neurotic doesn't have to be all doom and gloom. After all, worrying about our health is what keeps us taking vitamins and visiting the doctor's office for checkups. In that case, neurotics may actually be one step ahead.

The Big Five Winning Formula

If the human psyche has been narrowed down to five key components, does it follow that there's a winning formula? Is there an ideal combination of traits that every human being should possess to be truly happy?

The answer is yes and no.

It certainly appears that some traits do make you happier than others. Some traits may even make you live longer. But personality is complex, and new scientific discoveries continue to emerge that often challenge preexisting views. Personality can also change over time, so the extent to which people can optimize themselves and cultivate the ideal combination of traits—if it exists—may be limited. But if you're willing to try, here are some hacks that may help.

Don't Want to Be Sick? Try Being More Extroverted.

As a child, did you love to get dirty? Did you get mud all over yourself without any thought to germs—or who was going to do the laundry? Don't tell your own kids or you could be stuck washing clothes for the next three weeks, but you may have actually been on to something. As it turns out, some germs are good for you, and the more you're exposed to them, the more your body gets used to dealing with them.

According to a study led by Professor Kavita Vedhara, extroverts were linked to an increased expression of pro-inflammatory genes, while people ranking high in conscientiousness were associated with a lower expression of these genes. In other words, people ranking higher on the extrovert scale were biologically less susceptible to disease.

That's where being more extroverted can help you. The more people you see, the more you're exposed to a bigger network of germs and possible infections, and the more your body learns to cope. While practicing good hygiene is important, some bacteria can actually toughen up our bodies to diseases.

On the other hand, the more time you spend alone, the less prepared your body is to battle new germs once they come. Being too clean could actually hurt you. The size of your circle of friends, therefore, could actually be a good indicator of the strength of your immune system.

So if you want to be sick less often, try being more extroverted. That means trying to be more comfortable around others and opening yourself up to greater social opportunities. Think of people as germs—you need exposure to some if you're going to stay healthy!

You can start by practicing short conversations with strangers. Next time you visit your local coffee shop, ask your server how their day is going. When you take a taxi, ask your cab driver if it's been a busy night. The more you practice starting conversations, the more natural it will feel and the easier it will become.

Once you've got the gift of the gab, go out and use it. Say yes to dinner invitations you would normally refuse or invite your friends over to your house more often. Stay off your cell phone in public and see if there's an opportunity to meet someone while you're on the street or waiting for the bus. Sign up for your local Toastmasters club and practice public speaking with other people who also want to improve.

It can be nerve-racking at first to step outside of your comfort zone. But if you take baby steps, set yourself incremental goals, and accept any failures as lessons on the path to success, you could be setting yourself up for a more extroverted—and healthier—future in no time.

Want to Live Longer? Be More Conscientious.

When you go on vacation, are you the type to fly by the seat of your pants and book nothing but the plane ticket there? Or do you prefer to know where you're staying, how you'll get there, and what you'll be doing every day thereafter until you return home?

If you're the former, you may be seeking out more excitement in the short term but, in reality, cutting back your adventure in the end. That's because people who are more conscientious—that is, they are more organized and prefer planning over spontaneity—are actually known to live longer.

According to a 75-year longitudinal study by Joshua Jackson (2015), which followed a group of couples in their mid-20s, men with higher levels of conscientiousness were found to live longer. That's because people high in this trait were more organized, self-disciplined, and prepared. They did fewer things that were spontaneous and more things that were safer. Conscientiousness, therefore, helped them reach riper old ages.

So it turns out that safety pays off. On top of being more organized, high-conscientious people are more self-disciplined and dependable. Even where they dream of taking risks, they convince themselves that it's not in their best interests They stick to their plans and, as a result, do fewer potentially life-threatening things.

If you want to live longer, you could try to be more conscientious. First, get organized about your tasks and your priorities. These days, there are lots of apps that can help you manage your time.

Once you know what needs to be done, you can train yourself to better focus on achieving it. Try meditating for even 10 minutes a day. You may find that, over time, you're distracted less and concentrating more on the tasks at hand.

Finally, remember that you don't need to go cold turkey. One step at a time, you may find yourself living a more mindful, determined, and possibly even longer life.

Want a Healthier Heart? Be More Agreeable.

When you're in a good mood, how do you—your body, that is—feel? Does it feel light and energetic, or does it feel heavy and tired? The odds are that when you're in a good mood, so is your body.

As it turns out, the saying that good things happen to good people might actually be true. People who rank high on the agreeableness scale—that is, they're friendly, more compassionate, and looking to get along with everyone—do in fact have healthier hearts versus their more pessimistic peers.

What's the science behind it? According to Bibbey (2013), the less agreeable you are, the weaker your biological stress reactivity—or how your body manages stress. The more relaxed and optimistic you are, and the more you're able to take things in stride, the less stress there is on your heart. That means a healthier heart will keep beating longer. Being more agreeable, therefore, means that your heart is in a much better state.

Now, there are several steps you can take to be more agreeable. First, when you wake up in the morning, tell yourself that you're going to be agreeable with every single person you talk to that day. Go out of your way to be nice to people and to actively listen to them.

Second, try getting involved in volunteer work. Spend some time at your local charity. Seeing those less fortunate than us can bring a better perspective on our own lives.

Finally, practice the art of compromise. If you're adamant about something going your way, you may be alienating everyone else who's involved. But if you're willing to show understanding and put the interest of others above your own, you may just be building a more solid social network to support you down the road.

It may seem hard, but being more agreeable is really just about being more empathetic and less combative with the people you come across. Trying to bring a little more pleasantness, decency, and humbleness to your demeanor can work wonders not only on your social life, but also on your health.

Want to be Happier? Be More Open to Experience.

The last time you tried something new, how did you feel? Maybe it was eating sushi for the first time or taking a dance class. Chances are, even if you didn't like it, you were proud of yourself for taking that step. As it turns out, it may be worth taking a few more of those steps. People who are more open to experience might just be happier overall.

What's the reason? Open people are by nature more curious. Sensitive to beauty, they have a deeper appreciation for art. They're also more in tune with their emotions, and they think and act in ways that may not necessarily conform to society. All of that is to say that they seek out things that make them happy.

At the end of the day, trying new things is good for us. But being open to experience doesn't have to mean jumping out of planes.

There are several ways you can discover new things that don't put your life at risk.

First, recognize where your comfort zone is and then step outside of it. Do you like exercising but are afraid of going to the gym? Try a low-key yoga class to get started.

Second, don't worry about what the world around you will think. Have you always wanted to try online dating but were too afraid? Just think, everyone else you'll meet is doing the exact same thing.

Finally, remember that life is short. You may wind up regretting all the things you never tried when it's too late to start.

Being more open to experience can bring you more of the things you've always wanted—and happiness along the way.

Want to Be More in Control? Try Being a Little Less Neurotic.

When was the last time you second-guessed yourself? That never-ending cycle of doubt, wondering if you made the right choice, was likely worse punishment than either choice you could have made. Neuroticism can lead people to do many things, but at the heart of it is the inability to control your thoughts and emotions. Being a little less neurotic may just give you a little more control over yourself, your actions, and, in the end, your overall well-being.

Neurotic people are intense, emotionally speaking. They respond to things in ways that most people wouldn't. They're prone to seeing the challenge, the hopelessness, and the threat that lies in everyday situations. Their negative reactions can go on for longer than others, leaving them in frequent bad moods.

Neurotic people can be prone to vulnerability, leaving them panicked, confused, and helpless under stress. They can suffer intense anxiety and live with a constant fear of something dangerous happening. And they can be sensitive to the perceived judgments of others, leaving them shy, uncomfortable, and even ashamed.

When they're in that state, it can be hard to think clearly, to know what to do, and to handle the situation effectively. That can be a challenging and very likely unhealthy way to live.

On the other hand, if you're able to maintain your calm, poise, and confidence when you're stressed, you become less vulnerable to outside stress. You're less anxious about what may happen next and you're able to embrace the unknown instead of fear it. You're also not worried about other people watching or judging you.

So how do you become less neurotic?

It may sound grim, but start by reflecting on your own mortality. Once you realize you won't be around forever—and neither will anyone else—you can start to chip away at your neuroses and focus on enjoying the moment.

Next, work out. Exercise can release chemicals in the brain that boost your mood and can go a long way to helping you deal with any anxiety.

Finally, recognize your triggers and try to avoid them. If the same person or situations are always making you anxious or stressed, the easiest solution is to avoid them. Find people and places that help you relax.

Being a little neurotic can be a good thing. But if you find you're not as in control of your emotions as you'd like, challenging your neuroses could lead you to a better, more relaxed state of mind.

Takeaways:

- The Big Five personality traits are one of the first attempts to classify people based on specific traits rather than as a whole. You can remember the traits easily with the acronym OCEAN: openness to experience (trying new things), conscientiousness (being cautious and careful), extroversion (drawing energy from others and social situations),

agreeableness (warm and sympathetic), and neuroticism (anxious and high-strung).
- Unlike other assessments in this book, there have actually been determined to be a winning formula for these traits—not per se, but if you display certain traits, you are more likely to have better mental health and increased happiness. If you are more of the first four traits (OCEA) and less neurotic, you will tend to be happier and more fulfilled in life. It's not hard to understand why—you'll have more experiences, you'll live longer from your caution, you'll have a wider social circle and support system, you'll get along better with others, and you'll be less anxious and more relaxed.

Chapter 3. Myers, Briggs, and Keirsey

There are a lot of different personality tests out there. This chapter will explore the Myers-Briggs Type Indicator (MBTI) as well as the subsequent Keirsey Temperaments. These temperaments were a result of the MBTI to help organize it better and create more relatable classifications and categories.

The MBTI has also been one of the most popular ones for people to use when conceiving of personality. It's highly doubtful that people haven't heard of this test, as many have taken various forms of it without even knowing. Overall, the test is based on four very distinct *dichotomies*, which you can imagine as simply being traits. People have compared the MBTI as one that purely functions as a modern horoscope. The thing to remember, though, is that this doesn't mean it's no longer beneficial.

The MBTI was developed around the time of World War II. Myers and Briggs were two housewives and observed many people taking job opportunities. However, it bothered them that many of those people were taking jobs that didn't necessarily pertain to their skills.

These two were also very interested in the theories and works of Carl Jung, a Swiss psychiatrist. Jung believed that archetypes came from models of people, behavior, and their personalities. He strongly suggested that these archetypes came innately due to the influence of human behavior. Overall, he concluded that people inherit these archetypes in the same manner that they inherit instinctive patterns of behavior.

Because of Jung's theories and influence, the MBTI was developed. Myers and Briggs's intention was to produce a useful enough test that geared specifically toward women heading into the workforce. The goal was to give them this test to help them find job assignments that were most suitable and aligned with their personalities.

The MBTI and Personality Types

Carl Jung theorized that people and their psychological types could be characterized by general traits along three spectrums.

For personality, the spectrum has at two ends: extroverted (E) versus introverted (I).

For perception, the spectrum has at two ends: sensing (S) versus intuition (N).

Then, for judging, the spectrum has at two ends: thinking (T) versus feeling (F).

These three areas of preferences were introduced as dichotomies by Jung. These dichotomies were considered to be bipolar dimensions where each of the poles represented different preferences. Utilizing this proposal by Jung, Myers suggested that the judging-perceiving relationship was the fourth dichotomy for influential personality types—judging (J) versus perceiving (P).

The idea is that everyone can measure themselves along these four spectrums, and certain patterns will emerge so that you are able to discover your personality type.

The first criterion, extraversion versus introversion, signifies the source as well as the direction of a person's energy expression.

An extrovert and his energy expression mainly happens in the external world. When in the presence and company of others, extroverts are able to recharge. For an introvert, his source of energy mainly happens in his internal world. Having space to himself or herself is ideal and can prove to be the best mode of recharging that energy expression.

Extroverted people are action-oriented in comparison to introverted people, who are more thought-oriented. In a classroom, extroverted students like to participate in group discussions and presentations. Their interactions with other students provide that sense of charge for their personality types. An introverted student would rather work alone on projects and feel somewhat uncomfortable during whole class discussions. They like being able to think on their own and work through assessments by themselves as well.

The second criterion, sensing versus intuition, represents how someone perceives information.

When a person is sensing, he or she believes information received directly from that external world. This may come in the form of using his or her five senses—sight, smell, touch, taste, and hearing. Decisions come in more immediate and practical ways.

For someone using intuition, he or she believes information from an internal world - their intuition, over external evidence. This comes in the form of having that "gut feeling." He or she digs a little deeper into detail and tries to connect patterns. It may take a little longer before a decision can be made.

Sensing has to do with believing information that is more concrete and tangible over intuition, which is more about looking at the underlying theories or principles that may come out of data. A police officer will always use evidence and data to support their claims for making an arrest because this information is measurable. On the other side, a lawyer would exhibit more intuition because there could be a lot more to the context being presented, which helps him defend his clients.

The third criterion, thinking versus feeling, has to do with how a person processes information. Thinking is when someone makes a decision mainly through the process of logical thinking. They also think in tangible means, where they look to rules to guide their decision-making.

Opposite to this is the feeling where someone would rather make a decision based on emotion. For decisions, these people look to what they value as a means for choosing their best option. They may deem thinkers as being cold and heartless.

Thinking mostly occurs when someone lays out all the possible and practical reasons for making a sound decision. Basically, someone is going to make a decision using one's brain. Feeling is when someone will make that decision from the heart. People who purchase homes will either sign the paperwork based on pricing and resale value (thinking) versus those buying to stay in their old neighborhoods (feeling).

The fourth criterion, judging versus perceiving, is how someone will implement the information he has processed.

Organizing life events is how someone would judge and later use it, as a rule, to stick to the plan. These people like to have order and structure. Their sense of self-control comes from being able to control their environments as much as possible. Judging types will normally use previous experiences as a catalyst to either continue or avoid certain behaviors later. They also like to see things settled and done with.

Improvisation and option exploration is what someone would do with perceiving. These people like having options and see organization being a limit to their potential. They like to make choices when they are necessary and like to explore problem-solving and strategizing. Perceiving types will somewhat live in the moment and understand that there are multitudes of options available to them, regardless of how other experiences have occurred in the past.

There are a total of 16 different combinations, or personality types, that can come out of the permutations of preferences in the mentioned four dichotomies. These help to represent one of the two poles that each person can have in terms of a dominant dichotomy. So this is what defines the 16 different personality types, as each can be assigned a four-letter acronym. These are the corresponding combinations:

The first letter corresponds to the first letter preference of general attitude.
E: extraversion or I: introversion

The second letter corresponds to the preference within the dimension of sensing-intuition.
S: sensing or N: intuition

The third letter corresponds to the preference within the pair of thinking-feeling.
T: thinking or F: feeling

The fourth letter corresponds to the preference within the pair of judging-perceiving.
J: judging or p: perception

So for instance, ISTP would stand for introverted, sensing, thinking, and perceiving. These individuals might be those daredevils always looking for their next adventure and contemplating this over a bottle of their favorite recreational beverage.

ESFJ would stand for extroverted, sensing, feeling, and judging. These people might be those you see on television sitcoms who gossip about everyone and whose main goal in life is to be married with kids, only to be able to gossip with other moms around the neighborhood.

The point scores on each can also vary from person to person, even those considered to be the same personality type. This shares similarities with the Big Five personality traits, and functions in the same vein of applying specific traits to people.

Shortcomings of the MBTI

Although the test provides insight into one personality, it does have some shortcomings that make it difficult to rely on all of its data.

For one, the 16 types described are only stereotypes. This means that they don't necessarily describe the individuals. Stereotypes, in their own way, are not the ideal ways to judge anyone. They never represent an entire population, so it becomes a slippery slope when trying to use it in categorizing others.

Another shortcoming is that the descriptions for each only appear to be accurate because of the Forer effect, also known as the Barnum effect (1956). The Barnum effect is where people have a tendency to conform to generalized statements if they are supposedly about them—people will look for what they are told and what they want, even if it is barely there. Fortune tellers and astrologers use this method to prove to their customers that they have this "paranormal gift."

People who like to use their horoscopes as ways of leading their lives are perfect examples of those who utilize the Barnum effect. They read through the descriptions for each day, study the behaviors of their own signs, and, in a sense, create a reality for themselves and believe it has to do with what they've read and studied.

Although this is naturally a human trait, it doesn't help to explain the typology or results of the MBTI test. This is because the Barnum effect was based purely off people's responses alone.

Another shortcoming is that the MBTI only gives answers that are definitive, and it doesn't account for the fact that people are usually not one-sided on their traits. People aren't entirely on one end of the spectrum over another. The MBTI only gives people two ends of the spectrum, not anything in between. Thus, most people can be moderate in many other traits.

For instance, you might be 45% extroverted and 55% introverted, but the MBTI would call you an introvert without subtlety.

Lastly, the MBTI's reliability is poor because it claims that each personality type is inborn and remains with people throughout their lives. A researcher, David Pittenger, studies that when a test-retest interval is done over a short amount of time, as many as 50% of people will get classified into a different type.

Rightly so, Pittenger also observed that this occurs due to the fact that there are cutoff points diving the dimensions. This issue can be seen by the geographical analogy mentioned—small changes at the boundaries, where most people will be, are able to produce a huge change in the overall result.

Over time and as expected, people can change. Results from their MBTI can change in a span of either days or weeks depending on their moods or influences from their external and internal environments. These factors will say nothing about their actual personality types.

Keirsey's Temperaments Sorter

One of the other popular ways of understanding the MBTI is through David Keirsey's four temperaments. He helped to organize the information people received from MBTI to narrow it down from 16 personality types to four general temperaments instead. Within each temperament Keirsey also identified two types of roles one might play instinctively and naturally.

The Four Temperaments

"The Guardian"
This happens when someone results in being a sensor and judger. These people have a longing to belong, contribute to their society, and are confident in their own abilities.

Guardians are also concrete are more organized. They seek security and belonging while still being concerned with responsibilities and duties. Logistics is one of their greatest strengths; they are excellent at organization, facilitation, supporting, and checking. Their two roles are administrators and conservators.

Administrators tend to be the proactive and directive versions of guardians. They are most efficient in regulating and their attentive inspectors and supervisors are their highest role variants. Conservators are the reactive and expressive versions of guardians and their best intelligence is supporting.

"The Artisan"
This occurs when an individual tests as being a sensor and perceiver. These individuals live

freely and through a lot of action-filled events.

Artisans are completely adaptable. They usually seek out stimulation and virtuosity. Artisans are highly concerned with making a large impact, and one of their greatest strengths happens to be tactics. They are extremely proficient in troubleshooting, problem-solving, and agility. They also have the ability to manipulate tools, instruments, and equipment.

Artisans have two roles—operators and entertainers. Operators are the directive and proactive version of artisans. They have a high capacity to expedite and are the attentive crafters and promoters of the role variants. Entertainers are the more informative and reactive versions of artisans. They have a great way of improvising and are the attentive to details.

Keirsey estimates that about 80% of the population is categorized as being artisans or guardians.

"The Idealist"

This happens when someone results in being an intuitive and feeler. These people find meaning in their lives while helping themselves and others be the best versions of themselves. They value uniqueness and individuality.

Idealists are abstract and can be compassionate. They work to seek significance and meaning in almost everything. They are concerned with their own personal growth and being able to find their true identities. They are very good at diplomacy and have strengths in clarifying, unifying, individualizing, and inspiring others. They have two roles—mentors and advocates.

Mentors are the proactive and directive versions of Idealists. They are very good at developing and their attentive variant roles are counselors and teachers. Advocates are the reactive and informative idealists who are very good at mediating.

"The Rational"

This occurs when someone tests as being an intuitive and thinker. There is always a drive to increase these people's knowledge and they are highly competent. They usually have a sense of personal satisfaction.

Rationals are objective and abstract. They seek to be masters of their craft and have self-control. They are usually concerned with their own type of knowledge and competence. Strategy is their greatest strength, and they have the ability to logically investigate, engineer, conceptualize, theorize, and coordinate. Their two roles are coordinators and engineers.

Coordinators are the proactive and directive versions of rationals. They are great at arranging and their variant roles are masterminds and field marshals. Engineers are the reactive and informative versions of rationals.

Like the MBTI, Keirsey's temperament sorter has the ability to determine personality type based on four elements in people—energy or stimulant to a person, how people process information, make decisions, and tend to live their lives. Both tests allow a person to rate themselves based on a series of statements.

But they also differ when it comes to interpretation. Keirsey's assessment looks at the relation between each personality characteristic versus the MBTI focusing on each one individually. Keirsey personalities are also grouped by how people see the world while the MBTI prioritizes how people relate to other people. The MBTI might be a more accurate account because how people relate to others is much more intimate and reliable than how they see the world, which can be full of stereotypical factors.

When it comes to the four different temperaments, Keirsey and MBTI have specific ways of analyzing the data for people's personality traits.

First, how people interact with others will look different between the MBTI and Keirsey tests. Extroverted people would prefer to spend time collaborating with others and sharing ideas through MBTI's interpretation.

Keirsey would describe these people as being expressive and energized when they're in contact with others.

MBTI would describe Introverted people as those preferring to spend time alone, drawing on their own thoughts. Keirsey would say that these people are reserved and find energy in being alone. They do like to socialize but in more intimate settings.

Second, take how people process information and the world around them as an example, here.

MBTI would interpret a sensing person to prefer their reliance on senses when gathering and evaluating information. Keirsey's interpretation of this same individual would be that he or she is an observer and pays more attention to the outside world. He or she would seek out facts to make an overall judgment.

For Intuition, MBTI would say that these people rely on their instincts by using abstract thinking whereas Keirsey would say that these people enjoy introspection and enjoy daydreaming. Sometimes, they'll end up missing a lot of what's going on around them.

An example would be the difference between a journalist for a newspaper and a blog writer on a personal webpage.

Third, when it comes to governing decision-making, MBTI would say that thinking people prefer to make decisions carefully and weighing out all of their options prior to doing so. On the Keirsey assessment, these people would drive their decisions by logic and hide their emotions because they may be embarrassed by intense feelings that could potentially go out of control.

When it comes to feeling, MBTI would say these people prefer to make decisions instantly through their emotions. Keirsey interprets these people as valuing the importance of feelings over logic and following their hearts.

And for the fourth, when it comes to organizing their lives, MBTI would indicate that judgment people would prefer to have control in their surroundings so they can anticipate what comes next. Keirsey would describe these people as being schedulers and have a strong desire for structure.

People who score perception on the Myers-Briggs test would like the flexibility to explore all of their options in order to learn from them. Keirsey would interpret these same people as probers who are less likely to tie themselves down to a schedule since they are so open to alternative options. An instance of this would be the difference between a highly organized event planner and a traveling musician.

Keirsey's temperament sorter has the ability to take personality trait assessment a few steps deeper than that of MBTI. It helps to evaluate a person's results as it relates to other traits while MBTI focuses on each trait individually. But like MBTI, no individual can ever be just one temperament. Almost every single person will have traits in all temperaments, so it would be extremely difficult to pinpoint just one category.

Temperaments overall have the ability to give people a better sense into how they are and what they can do to change their personalities. Being a personality type merely tells someone how they are, but temperaments look beyond that surface level interpretation. Temperament identification allows people to score themselves and potentially make a change for the better. They have more self-awareness about themselves and can better adapt if needed.

Both tests have the ability to test people's personalities, but careful considerations should be made when evaluating the results. Each test will yield particular results that have more priority over another. In the end, nothing definitive may have been discovered except a helpful template to guide your life decisions.

Takeaways:

- The MBTI, though helpful as a guideline, can sometimes suffer from people treating it like a horoscope and reading into their

type what they wish to see about themselves.
- The MBTI functions on four distinct traits and how much of each trait you are or are not. The traits are generally introverted/extroverted (your general attitude toward others), intuitive/feeling (how you perceive information), thinking/feeling (how you process information), and perceiving/judging (how you implement information). Thus, this creates 16 distinct personality types.
- The MBTI does suffer from some shortcomings, including the lack of subtlety when most people are a bit of each trait, the usage of stereotyping to classify people, and the lack of consistency when people score differently depending on their current moods and circumstances.
- The Keirsey temperaments were a way of organizing the same information gleaned from the MBTI. Here, there are four distinct temperaments, each with two types of roles, instead of 16 personality types. The four temperaments are guardian, artisan, idealistic, and rational.

Keirsey himself estimated that up to 80% of the population fell into the first two temperaments.

Chapter 4. Unconscious Upbringings

This chapter works to discuss how people's upbringing have direct influence and effect to their personalities, especially in the subconscious manner. Not all of this may be true, but it's safe to say that there is a plethora of research that has yielded some very interesting theories. These tell researchers that it's worth looking into people's childhoods to find clues as to why people act the way they do.

Alfred Adler Birth Order Theory

One theory that doesn't have much scientific validation to back it up is the Alfred Adler birth order theory. This proposed theory came from Alfred Adler (1870–1937) as he studied the effect that birth order had on people's personality. By definition, birth order was the order of when a child was born in his or her given family.

For instance, in a family of three, the sequence goes as follows:

The first child is the first born.
The second child is the middle born.
The youngest child is the later or third born.

You may agree at first glance that birth order does seem to create a certain personality type. There's the stereotype that the eldest child must set the example for the other children and has the most pressure from parents to succeed in a conventional manner. That of course means the younger children are allowed to run wild because there is less pressure. This may be true, but the idea of birth order becomes a bit more complex when consideration is placed on the effects of birth order on children's personalities.

According to Adler, the first-born children would receive a lot of attention from the family. But that attention would last only up until the second child was born. Once the second child came into the picture, the first child would be considered Adler's coined term "dethroned." All of these actions unconsciously influenced the child's personality through adulthood.

First Born
Let's take a look at the first child. Adler stated that they will be prone to perfectionism and a constant need for affirmation or validation. This would then translate to them being intellectual, conscientious, and dominant in most social settings. Adler would describe this child as losing his parent's devoted attention with the presence of other children, and he would try to get it back somehow, even if it took his entire life in doing so.

This same child would have expectations set to be a role model for the younger siblings.

This child has control of attention from the parents because there is no one else to compete with. Once control of attention is lost on the first child's part, he can have one or several of the following reactions:

- protects himself against forces that can change his destiny
- becomes insecure or extremely conservative
- helps parents when the second child is born

Second Born
Then there are the second born and middle children. Adler's perspective on second-born children was that they grow up sharing attention from caregivers of the first born. Since they grew up learning to share this attention, they're more likely to cooperate and be less needy than first-born children.

Second-born children are able to follow examples set by older siblings. They are usually trying to follow in the footsteps of the eldest children and catch up to them. Because of this, Adler believed that second-born children are more likely to adjust to life in general than the other children. This child is also prone to being dethroned if another child is born afterward.

Adler refers to the second born as the "pacemaker." Because the first born came before her, this might prompt her to be competitive, rebellious, and always wanting to be the best at everything. She might struggle with trying to figure out her place in the family, then later in the world.

Second-born children are eager for praise from their parents, and from this, and they often develop keen traits in arts or academia to compensate for this goal. If they are the middle children, they tend to be more flexible and diplomatic than other members of the family.

Last Born
These children are the babies of the family. The baby can never be dethroned by another sibling. They don't really have any followers but can be considered antagonistic toward other siblings because they become the

center of attention for an extended number of years without competition.

Typically, the baby will get most of the attention in families. This is large fact due to the other siblings moving on in their stages of life. They will have developed their own sense of independence without having to rely on their parents. Thus, this results in leaving all of the attention to the youngest child, the last born.

According to Adler, the youngest child also tends to be dependent and selfish. This happens because they have always been taken care of by other family members and not necessarily through any fault of their own. The last born can also possess positive traits such as confidence, socializing, and the ability to have fun. They are the only children who don't have to fight for attention from their parents.

They will, though, have difficulty with authority, especially when they are told no. Going to school is a hard transition because they have to shift their focus to the teacher.

Adler did express that these children would be more mature and feel more comfortable around others versus other children.

Only Child
So what about the only child? This is the one type that is still difficult to completely evaluate when it comes to the development of personality types. Researchers have indicated the only child has tendencies to develop first-born characteristics. Others have said that an only child could be classified in any of the birth order personalities. For instance, the only child can have the same characteristics as the middle child or the last born.

When it comes to birth order, it's not a matter of choice and subconscious. It can affect people's identities simply from the basis of chance and when someone is born in the family. Because of this, it allows people to gauge a better understanding into who they are and why they act the way they do based on their order in their families.

Attachment Theory

Attachment theory is another theory where unconscious happenings during childhood affect people well into adulthood.

Based on research started by John Bowlby, notably continued by Mary Ainsworth, then by Bartholomew and Horowitz, there are four main attachment styles, or ways we approach emotional attachment to other people. These patterns usually begin with children's relationships to their parents or caretakers and persist into adulthood where they influence adult relationships.

According to Bowlby, the theory essentially forces the child to unconsciously ask whether the caretaking figure is nearby and attentive. If the child perceives the answer to this question to be yes, he will feel loved, secure, and confident. As a result, the child will feel confident to explore and have a degree of physical and mental separation from the caretaker. However, if the child perceives the answer to be no, the child will experience anxiety and become fearful whenever the caretaker is not in their immediate vicinity.

These feelings form the basis for the attachment styles.

The four attachment styles are:

1. Secure
2. Anxious-preoccupied
3. Dismissive-avoidant
4. Fearful-avoidant

Secure Attachment

As much as we would like to think that secure attachment is the most common attachment style, it absolutely is not. And there's a reason the other three attachment styles have somewhat ominous names.

People with secure attachment styles are emotionally balanced and have a history of warm and caring interactions that began in childhood. They don't approach people out of fear. Instead they have a strong sense of self and look for the positive in any relationship.

They have a healthy range of positive and negative emotions and are less prone to emotional outbursts because they are secure. They may be independent or relatively dependent, but it's a conscious choice and not based on anxiety or fear.

They aren't emotionally repressed and can express their emotional closeness and attachment with little or no trouble. Securely attached people feel comfortable with intimacy. They do not view it as a threat. They do not feel that intimacy is completely dependent on their partner or that it robs them of their independence. Instead, they understand that when they enter into a relationship, a third party is born—the relationship.

Not surprisingly, these people are able to be warm and loving. Again, love is defined as you giving, not taking. Anxious people define love as taking.

The biggest difference between securely attached people and other types of people is their lack of insecurity. This allows them to open themselves to others yet give others space when it is needed.

How do they act in relationships?

Just imagine how someone who is secure and confident in their relationship acts. They are not jealous or possessive and they don't have nightmares about being cheated on. They are attentive but relaxed and generally allow independence and freedom because they don't feel they have anything to worry about.

Various studies report that people with this attachment style are happier and more fulfilled in their relationships, and that's no surprise. Imagine what a relationship where the sanctity of the relationship was never in question would be like. Some people never get to that point.

If you want this chapter to be anything more than a series of "Oh, that's interesting" moments, you should take a moment to honestly assess how much each of these attachment styles resonates with you. Don't make the mistake of assuming that your attachment style is automatically secure or healthy.

If you don't take the time to diagnose yourself, and you subsequently attempt to remedy or fix a problem with your relationships, it's like taking a random medication to treat an illness. It doesn't make sense to do that. And yes, loving others does indeed start with loving yourself.

Anxious-Preoccupied Attachment

This is the first type of insecure attachment, and it is defined by anxiety and preoccupation with the relationship.

People with this attachment style tend to fixate on whether their partner loves them as much as they love their partner. It is a constant source of anxiety for them because they can never be adequately reassured.

Every small sign that could possibly be interpreted as negative is unequivocally negative to them and causes them significant mental anguish. They tend to measure this on a daily basis, which causes undue stress.

At the heart of it, people with this attachment style are very insecure and don't regard themselves in a very positive light. They doubt that their partner is able to love them as much as they want and deserve. There is an inferiority complex at work here, and constant validation is required in any and all forms—phone calls, texts, physical contact, attention, eye contact.

Their anxiety goes into remission when they are in close contact with their paramour, so they naturally want more and more.

Interestingly, they focus mainly on the love they are receiving, not the love they are giving to their partner. This is a serious problem because the classic definition of love, of course, is a person giving.

By many accounts, true love is measured by what you give, what you sacrifice, and the emotional value you give to another person. This begs the question—do people with this attachment style feel true love, or is a relationship merely a vehicle to validate their self-worth?

How do they act in relationships?

Just as you think they might. Like my aunt, they will be uneasy when their partner is out of their sight or they have lost contact with them for a few hours. They need constant affirmation in all forms—verbal and physical. They can tend to get jealous and possessive because they feel anxious if anything appears to threaten their relationship.

Dismissive-Avoidant Attachment

Dismissive-avoidant people are focused on their independence.

They are afraid that once they get into a relationship, they will become saddled with duties and obligations and lose control of their life. They are happy with the fact that they are able to make choices in the first place and are fierce about protecting that privilege. They conflate deep levels of emotional intimacy with a loss of independence and control.

To that effect, they don't feel the need for close emotional relationships because they appear to do more bad than good for them. They characterize themselves as islands or lone wolves by choice.

Their very predictable response is to minimize closeness. They come up with arrangements to keep people at arm's length. It is not uncommon for dismissive-avoidant people to set ground rules that prevent the relationship from truly maturing.

They may accept sexual or physical intimacy, but avoidant people take great pains to minimize true emotional closeness. Unsurprisingly, they can be seen as cold or callous sometimes.

It is not because they do not love the other person. They are afraid that love will rob them of their independence, so they choose different priorities. They don't lack empathy; they just don't let it dictate their actions.

People with this style of attachment sometimes suppress their emotions because of how independent they characterize themselves.

How do they act in relationships?

They have a very doubtful view of relationships, so it's unclear if you'd be able to get them into one. They have a strong fight-or-flight response—meaning that if things don't go their way, they will often prioritize themselves first and leave the relationship.

They can be very difficult to deal with for other attachment styles because their style of attachment is to *not* have attachment. When someone wants to remain by themselves, it can be a waste of time trying to introduce your needs to them. They are stubborn and unwilling to compromise for others because that represents exactly what they hate in relationships.

Ideally, they would be in a relationship with another dismissive-avoidant person and they would coexist peacefully within their own spaces. Be careful of encroaching on this person's space and forcing them into something.

Fearful-Avoidant Attachment

At first glance, this attachment style appears similar to the dismissive-avoidant.

But the dismissive-avoidant is motivated by very different things. They want to avoid emotional attachment because they feel attachments weaken them; it's a waste of time. Fearful-avoidant people avoid emotional attachment because they feel attachment only leads to heartbreak, disappointment, and feelings of abandonment. Recall that these attachment styles often have their roots in childhood, so people with this attachment style may have experienced childhood traumas or abuse; they may have been abandoned or betrayed by someone they wanted or needed to depend on.

Despite wanting intimate relationships and emotional connection, they have issues opening up and truly getting close to others because a defensive wall shoots up that has been necessary in the past. Vulnerability has hurt them before and they want to prevent that now and in the future.

They do not have a positive view of others and have trouble seeing others as particularly trustworthy. Even if you have no history of wrongdoing and say all the right things, you will be constantly scrutinized by people with this attachment style. They are masters of preemptively rejecting others before they have the possibility of being hurt by them.

Because they want to protect themselves at all costs, they are uncomfortable displaying affection, verbal or otherwise. They suppress any positive feelings to keep themselves within the moat of their castle.

How do they act in relationships?

It's hard to get them into one. And when you manage to, they will have trouble committing or opening up. It may take months or years to win their trust, something they don't give easily.

Constant affirmation and validation is necessary. Be careful not to show any signs of doubt or ambiguity because they might take that as the first sign they should bolt to protect themselves.

Different attachment types produce different relationships, and some attachment types are absolutely toxic when paired with others.

Take another moment to truly see what style you fit into it. If you fit into multiple, that's normal as well—but there is always going to be one dominant attachment style that characterizes you. Think about how your views toward attaching to others can drastically change how you act toward them. It might uncover subconscious biases or instances of self-sabotage to ease the discomfort associated with your attachment style.

For example, if you have a dismissive-avoidant person and an anxious-preoccupied person dating, what do you suppose will happen?

From the dismissive-avoidant person's perspective, they want to limit the amount of contact they have and maintain a very independent social life. They view their partner as a small sliver of their life and don't want to commit to obligations that would restrict them.

From the anxious-preoccupied person's perspective, the more points of contact the better. They can never be sure the other person still loves them, so they need to see them as much as possible to ensure they do. They seek commitment, but even a strong and explicit commitment won't stop their anxiety and constant need for validation.

It's not a match made in heaven. Uncovering your attachment style prevents a relationship built on misunderstandings. There's nothing we can do to change our circumstances in the past or our birth order. Unfortunately, they can have wide-ranging consequences on the people we grow into. But as always, nature doesn't have sole control of your personality.

Takeaways:

- An interesting subset of personality science is the ways people theorize we are influenced by our upbringings. Since this is largely while we were young children, this is said to be mostly unconscious and instinctual according to our early experiences.
- One theory is Adler's birth order theory, which states that the interaction between the first, middle, and youngest children in a family and how they compete for the affection and attention of the parents creates personality traits by themselves.
- The other prevailing theory on unconscious upbringings is attachment theory by Bowlby, which states that the way we view relationships with others is a direct result of how safe and secure we feel in regards to our caretakers as children. If you felt secure, you likely have secure attachment as an adult. If you felt less than secure, you could have any of the other three types of attachment: anxious-preoccupied, dismissive-avoidant, fearful-avoidant.

Chapter 5. Nurture Over Nature?

People may not realize it, but the environment around them has the ability to influence their personalities and identities. In fact, sometimes it is the ultimate factor. This is the other side of the nature versus nurture debate. With environment, you can make the argument that nurture is what ultimately takes control of someone's personality.

Although there is no clear answer here, there are compelling arguments that exist for both sides. This chapter works to explain how environment, nurture, and social and contextual influences can influence and shape people's identity and personality.

Many will argue that biology should be the determiner of personality and identity, but that's not something that people have the ability to influence. This is why there is less mentioning of it throughout the text. Instead, the focus is on people's environments and what people have the ability to change.

Social Learning Theory

Julian Rotter's social learning theory is one of the most popular theories that describe how people become who they become. Their identities are a result of their social learning tendencies as they observe and mimic others.

Claiming that personality is the representation of contact between a person and her environment is the main viewpoint behind Rotter's social learning theory. Thus, Rotter's theory poses that both the person and her environment should be considered in order to gain a full understanding of her behavior. People act a certain way, and this interacts with their environments, thus helping them learn from them. So this means there is a potential for change.

Rotter also notes that people are driven by their desire to pursue positive reinforcements while attempting to avoid negative reinforcements. In social learning environments, people will interact with others in a positive manner in the efforts of making new friends, networking, or working to move outside their comfort zones. If they were to act in rude ways, they'd expect to receive shun and negative feedback from others. In ways, these situations help to shape someone into who they are, especially around others.

What significance does this have, anyway? Well, being able to change one's environment is the first step in changing his way of thinking. Then this leads to a change in behavior, which reflects upon his personality traits changing to fit into that specific situation. People have the ability to observe and learn from people simply by watching them and attempting to emulate their behaviors.

Social theory aims to explain human behavior and the influences that people face in their everyday environments. When it comes to human behavior, it's most accurately predicted by understanding four variables: behavior potential, expectancy, reinforcement value, and psychological situation.

Behavior potential: This is where there's a possibility for a response in relation to its reinforcement.

Expectancy: This has to do with people's confidence that a particular reinforcement will evoke specific behavior. These are usually general or specific as the likelihood of success depends on either one.

Reinforcement Value: This happens when someone can foresee the type of reinforcement and place a preference on the more desirable one.

Psychological Situation: This part has to do with the external and internal world to which a person is responding. Behavior comes in the form of the interaction of people with their environments.

All of these variables integrate to what's known as the basic prediction formula. Basically, people can predict their own behavior, by which they evaluate their situations and understand the reinforcement that follows. For instance, a man seeking the attention of a woman he's attracted to might exhibit behaviors such as being chivalrous, nice, and attentive. He knows that, from the past, he's done this to get other women before, so it'll happen for him again.

Overall, Rotter's goal was to find how people function in reality in relation to their environments. Thus, this now put people in the driver's seat, so to speak, when it came to controlling their own personalities and identities.

Regional Personality Types

Believe it or not, there is real proof that regional personality types exist. This study was conducted primarily in the United States, in particular. This, alone, indicates that people's environments make a difference in their personalities. It's safe to say that on some level, people are just products of their surroundings.

In fact, in 2007, two psychology researchers, Michal Kosinski and David Stillwell, created a popular app, myPersonality, that would test people's personalities. They launched this app through Facebook, and nearly four million Facebook users utilized it.

Since this was such a large sample size and data was matched from Facebook profiles, it made it that much easier to evaluate a lot of the questions about personality differences that may have been previously inaccessible. All of the questions were different but they were still able to measure the Big Five personality traits as mentioned in a previous chapter. The study was able to find that there were big regional differences for each of the traits.

Another researcher, Jonah Sinick, decided to analyze the studies even further and was able to conclude the following.

Major party cities had high average numbers of extroverted people. What others would normally think is a traditional party city over a conservative hub would normally correspond to extraversion and introversion.

Seven out of 10 of the cities with highest average agreeableness were in Utah. Utah residents are almost 60% Mormon, which corresponds to the results. Mormons tend to have exceptionally high average agreeableness. One can even conduct a similar analysis to the one done previously for race and neuroticism.

Those New Yorkers are surely and unusually disagreeable. Eight out of the 10 cities listed somewhat directly relate to stereotypes given to New Yorkers—unfriendly, mean, aggressive, and rude. A survey from 2013 ranked New York City to be the sixth most unfriendly city in the world.

Low conscientiousness, or careful thought, went to the Bay Area. This came at a bit of a surprise considering cities like Berkeley, San Jose, San Francisco, Hayward, and Cupertino all made the list of 10 cities with low average conscientiousness. These all are cities that are simultaneously in the Bay Area.

Lastly, the artsy cities ranked highly with openness. Typically, openness is associated with artistic interests. So it made sense that Hollywood, Santa Fe, and New Orleans were considered areas where people were most open. They are known for being the most artistic, so their appearance at the top of the list is pretty spot on with expectations.

The influence of geographical location has an influence on people and their personalities. Depending on city priorities and culture, residents of those cities can differ simply because of their environments.

Culture and Nurture

It's pretty clear that people that come from different cultures will be different in their personalities. In her book *The Chrysanthemum and the Sword: Patterns of Japanese Culture,* Ruth Benedict included a detailed description of the Japanese belief and value system. Benedict also included a hypothesis that revealed the reason behind Japanese actions during World War II.

The book also speaks about the differences between guilt and shame in cultures. The distinction between the two as methods of social control was what Benedict described as American society (guilt) and Japanese society (shame).

In American society and cultural anthropology, guilt culture is when an individual is socially controlled when he or she fears to be undesirable. So society's emotion are used to sway individuals into compliance and obedience. A student who cheats on a test must deal with the guilt of doing something that is not only disallowed but frowned upon. In order to gain restitution, he must admit his wrongdoing and face the punishment. Guilt is an alternative in comparison to shame culture, which focuses more on pride and honor.

For Japanese society, social control comes from shaming others and making them feel ostracized for negative behavior. Guilt has to do with making someone anticipate consequences while shame makes people fearful of retribution. The same student who cheated on the test would have a different feeling with shame. He'd feel as though he let his family and teachers down by doing something that was dishonorable. Shame stresses self-denial and humility versus guilt stressing punishment and forgiveness.

Nature Versus Nurture

Finally, there is the debate about nature versus nurture. Although environments are important, there is still debate between which is more accurate and dominant. What exactly is the role of nature versus nurture and how does biology play a role in identities? Everything in this chapter thus far has proven the importance of nurture, but that's not the entire story.

Nurture references the environmental variables that impact who people are. This also includes their early childhood experiences, the way they were raised by their families, their social relationships, and the culture that surrounds them. Nature on the other hand has to do with all genes and hereditary factors. These influence who people are. From their physical appearances to their own personality characteristics, these factors play a very vital role.

For a stunning display of the influence of nature, a certain percentage of our modern population has something called the *Neanderthal quotient*.

23AndMe, a personal genome company, and many others like it have provided an index of how much overlap a person can have with DNA and the Neanderthals. Glenn Geher and others found that, on average, the population of those who have had their genomes mapped is at about 2.5%. This was according to research done by 23AndMe.

A good proportion of individuals are near the mean, and this variable tends to be distributed normally. It was rare to see that the scores were either much higher or lower than the mean. Thus, people would now be able to be assessed in terms of their NQ, also known as Neanderthal quotient.

There were about 200 participants in the study, which included adults from all over the world. They had already had their genomes mapped, reported their NQs, and completed a battery of psychological surveys in order to be tested for these predictions. With that being said, these are some of the highlights that were discovered—those who had scored high in NQ were found to be significantly high on dimensions of:
- Social fear
- Sociosexuality or promiscuity
- Depressive tendencies
- Bipolar tendencies
- Autistic tendencies

So when it comes to these dimensions, nature can indeed be different. Some people who are born with chemical imbalances in the brain literally have no control over some of their own behaviors.

But again, that's not the entire story. Take a person who is athletically inclined. Genetically, he would say that since his parents were athletes and great at basketball, he inherited those skills and motivation to be just like them. However, others would argue that his talent and determination came from constant practice and training, which is a result of his environment instead.

One can also examine a case of a woman who has high blood pressure and obesity. Would it be determined that she was born with her parents' health issues or was this something learned as she was growing up from other adults in her life, such as bad eating habits and poor exercise routines?

For nature, there are a few examples of biologically determined characteristics. These include things such as genetic diseases and hair, eye, and skin color. One could also expect other things such as life expectancy and height being strong components biologically. But all of these can still be influenced by environmental factors and lifestyle.

Most experts believe both nature and nurture have influence over behavior and development. More than ever, people are seeing and realizing that the simple notion of asking how much influence heredity and environment have over people's traits are not the best approaches to take. The reality is that there really is no simple way to pin it down to just one or the other. Influences on traits include more things such as genetic factors that interact with each other as well as environmental factors that interact with each other. This could look like social experiences and overall culture. It can also be a combination of both hereditary and environmental influences. It's more common to see researchers being interested in studying how genes modulate environmental influences and vice versa.

One instance of nature and nurture working together is through a set of twin siblings. Both grow up in the same household and carry the same genetic make-up from their parents. However, one grows up to be outgoing and friendly when he joins sports and other extracurricular activities while the other is more introverted and keeps to himself since he found more interests in academic studies and fine arts. Genetically, they have similar mannerisms and tendencies, but as they grew up, their environments changed their preferences and both chose to portray different traits.

Knowing all of this information, where do people go from here? Does it matter if nature or nurture is the reason for why people are the way they are? Not really. In fact, one can discover that a healthy balance between the two can be a more accurate and effective way of determining personality and identity. Knowing this helps people control their own environments and hereditary traits so they can focus on growth and happiness from there.

This also helps people really take a look at their current life situations and reflect on their positive and negative experiences. Then that analysis will shape their future choices based on what they have learned from their past and understanding of their own behavior and traits—whether those be from genetics or their environments.

Both of them matter and they can often work together. However, it's more possible for people to control their environments (nurture). Once people are more aware and conscientious of their surroundings and upbringing, they have more control over their behaviors and actions.

Takeaways:

- The age-old debate of nature versus nurture may never be settled definitively; rather, it should be said that they work together in all aspects of building one's identity.

- On the nurture side, social learning theory and the four variables (behavior potential, expectancy, reinforcement value, and psychological situation) give context to someone's identity. Regional and cultural differences also speak highly to the differences that a simple change in geography can cause in someone's identity.

- However, on the nature side, there has been shown to be a Neanderthal quotient measured in people who have very different personality traits from the rest of the population. The reality is that nature and nurture are intertwined too deeply and contribute equally to someone's adulthood identity.

Chapter 6. The Stories We Create

In this chapter, the focus is geared toward gaining insight about ourselves based on stories we might tell ourselves and what those stories might mean.

You might guess that this isn't as scientifically based as other chapters, and you would be exactly right. This is very similar to the chapter that talked about horoscopes, but it has a deeper and more detailed basis than that. Overall, it can be used as a guideline to discover personality and identity. Just don't build your hopes and dreams on it!

The overall goal here is to draw meaning from people's subconscious thought. When you ask yourself a pointed question (such as "What makes me happy?"), you likely aren't going to be able to answer that question. Even if you do answer the question, it probably won't be an answer that helps you achieve greater happiness.

There are two methods of interest: the Carl Jung personality test and Kate Wendleton's seven stories exercise. Both seek to evaluate personality based on answers that people give from seemingly innocent questions. Indeed, in a moment, you'll see why they can be seen like both a horoscope or an illuminating look into someone's psyche, depending on who you're talking to.

The Seven Stories Exercise

Kate Wendleton, career counselor, created this exercise out of Bernard Haldane's work in helping military personnel transition into civilian work.

After World War II in the 1940s, the job market began to get flooded with veterans returning home and looking for work. It was very evident that many businesses and organizations didn't possess the resources or skills to capitalize on these veterans' talents and capacities. Veterans were accustomed to jobs that pertained to war. These jobs weren't necessarily available or well known in the general labor force. They simply had no idea how to evaluate them.

Haldane wanted to do something to help the veterans. First, he asked veterans to recollect on their best achievements while at the same time clarifying what they enjoyed doing the most. Next, he helped them clarify their individual strengths and skills that were transferable. Specifically, the focus was to identify ones that could be useful to an employer.

Third, Haldane helped them market and present their offerings in a way that appealed to a potential employer. He would help the employer recognize the benefits of hiring the veterans based on their skills, achievements, and enjoyments.

Although it was deemed to be extremely radical at the time, Haldane's inside-out approach was able to help many veterans who needed assistance in seeking employment. He helped them find their strengths and skills that would eventually make them marketable in the conventional job market. Traditional methods for finding jobs always used an outside-in approach. In other words, old methods would try to fit people into job skills employers were looking for rather than highlighting on the individual's real skills to bring to the table.

Initially, Wendleton's exercise was created to help people in the realm of career counseling, but it's become popular to use when people want to identify the joys in their life. Also, it's used to help identify what people need more of in terms of the present and future. The ultimate goal is to help people discover exactly what they need in order to add more zest and joy to their overall lives.

The seven stories asks people to complete the following steps.

Step One: Write Down 25 Accomplishments

For this step, people would identify 25 accomplishments that they've felt good about doing. This would involve having people reflect on life accomplishments that ranged from childhood all the way to adulthood. The answers should be specific and not just a general statement. Normally, people may have a hard time with this, but they should really just go with their gut. They should write down whatever makes them feel good. Twenty-five is a lot of *anything* to think about, but the point is that you dig deep and leave no stone unturned.

For instance, someone might write that they were elected class president during their sophomore year in high school or they coordinated a charity fundraiser selling car wash tickets to benefit the homeless while in their junior year of college.

Step Two: Narrow That Down to Seven Accomplishments

From the list of 25, people should now narrow their list down to the seven most important and significant ones that have made them happy.

For most people, they may choose to elect ones such as overcoming cancer when they were 32 years old by actively going to treatment and changing their diets. They might also recall putting together their first furniture all on their own when first moving into their house. Typically, these seven accomplishments are more memorable and significant. Again, there is no definition or criteria for which seven you should use. Chances are you'll be able to figure out which are the most significant to you.

Step Three: Write Stories Associated with Those Seven Accomplishments

Taking from the seven narrowed accomplishments, people are to write out the stories that were associated with each of them. From here, they should be able to identify the skills and lessons learned and manifested from those experiences. They might be able to connect some dots and make connections to certain pathways that occurred during attainment of those accomplishments. Write the story in the first or third person and make sure to include the context and the aftermath of how you felt afterward.

When people are able to go through their experiences, they may be able to identify the elements of those experiences and how those elements made them happy. They can see commonalities in those experiences as well as certain aspects that attributed to their happiness. Write out the emotions felt in as much detail as possible and attempt to reflect in the story why there were such feelings of triumph and happiness.

Those who overcame cancer might talk about how they became much more optimistic in their outlooks on life as well as more resilient when faced with adversity. They remember those agonizing moments of chemotherapy but the great ways that the nursing staff helped them throughout the process. They saw the compassion that medical staff had for patients and, in turn, became more positive and uplifted.

For the people who put together furniture for the first time, they might recall feeling independent and able to follow directions once they really focused their attention to it. They remembered what it felt like to read through instructions that seemed like another language at first. They would also remember that great feeling of tightening that last screw and placing the furniture in the perfect spot in the house. It might sound trivial, but remember, it's about the feelings and emotions it gave you, not about the achievement itself.

Step Four: Analyze Those Stories

In a deeper purpose, people would now reflect and analyze what they learned from their experiences. Moreover, people can look back on all of her older experiences and attempt to connect them to ones pertaining to the seven stories.

Besides the cancer survivors learning about their feelings after the experience, they are now able to analyze their overall feeling of the process. They might discover that all of the experiences, even when negative, happened for a reason and they were meant to prosper through it all. They reminisce about all the things they used to love to do, like playing soccer or drawing, prior to being diagnosed with their condition. As a result, it motivates them to overcome this ailment and work toward participating in those hobbies again.

The homeowners may learn overall that they truly enjoy the beauty and struggles of homeownership. They start with a piece of furniture and then can feel confident to move onto bigger home projects like tile and floor replacements. They start to walk around the house and notice that the bathroom can get a little bit of a facelift. This motivation to do more because they loved the sense of accomplishment helps them power through their initial fear of not being a "do-it-yourselfer."

Step Five: 200 Possibilities to Achieve Goals

After people have determined what they're good at and love to do, they can come up with 200 possibilities that would help them carry out these activities. The purpose behind this is to help people get excited about their possibilities. They become more confident and not discouraged if one option doesn't always work out. Plus, it helps reduce people's attachment to just one possibility.

In terms of the cancer survivors, they'd be able to get excited about their newfound health and identify more steps they can take to stay healthy, such as regular screenings, healthy eating, and reduced exposure to toxins. Homeowners might think about enrolling in some DIY classes at the local hardware store to learn more about building things on their own.

The idea behind the seven stories is to get people to find ways to live their best lives possible based on what they have discovered and that they truly care about their lives. When people are able to reflect and identify things they've done well, and enjoyed them at the same time, it helps guide them in positive decision-making for their future. Knowing that they have a plethora of options and control over their own actions gives people the chance to be advocates in their own identities and behavior.

Carl Jung Personality Test

Another popular test used to test personality is that from Carl Jung. Carl Jung was normally very analytical and pluralistic in his thinking. He had a lot of influence from Buddhist ways of thinking, which then translated to the way he viewed and studied people and their personalities. He believed that there was a deeper connection to the way that people thought about simple things.

Although simple things are easier to identify, it's the answers that people provided that would reveal more about the person they were and how they prefer to do things. From how they view other people to how they envision their deaths, the questions from his personality test were very unique and intriguing. It's always been attributed to Carl Jung, but it seems to have gained a lot of popularity from the book *Diary* by Chuck Palahniuk.

The test asks individuals to answer the following.

First, name a color. Any color. Now think of three descriptive adjectives that describe that color.

Second, name an animal. Any animal. Now think of three descriptive adjectives that describe that animal.

Third, name a body of water. Name three descriptive adjectives describing it.

Fourth, imagine you're in a room. All the walls are white and there are no windows or doors. Describe in three descriptive adjectives how that room feels to you.

Stop here. Complete the questions. Then read on to see what they could mean about you.

The basis behind each question is where the evaluation and analysis really happens.

Question one: (color choice) the three words represent how you see yourself.
Question two: (animal choice) the three words represent how you see other people.
Question three: (body of water choice) the three words represent your preferred sex life.
The last question: (white room description) the three words represent your death.

Let's take a look at what each question and answer might be revealing. To reiterate, the answers you gave are not the important part; the adjectives you used are.

For instance, someone answers the following:
Teal: happy, cool, calming
Deer: timid, quiet, scared
Waterfall: raging, powerful, strong
White room: calm, tranquil, confusing

According to the test, this person sees themselves as happy, cool, and calming. Meanwhile, they see others as timid, quiet, and scared around them. They view sex as raging, powerful, and strong, and when they think of death, they think of calm, tranquility, and confusion.

Each of these questions has an interesting way of describing people based on the answers they provide. Although people believe they are just answering normal and easy questions, they are providing a deeper indication into who they are as a person.

Overall, this test asks people simple questions that they'd be able to answer, but it does provide a little more insight into the analysis of those answers. They are able to dissect the choices they make for each question and relate those answers to an evaluation of their personalities and identities. It's probably less scientific than anything else in this book, but it does provide food for thought and, at worst, is a great game to play with a date.

Both the seven stories exercise and the Carl

Jung personality test are methods that people can use to reflect and analyze their own experiences and behaviors. From there, they can better understand their own personalities and identities, which helps them become more self-aware. These tests can easily be used to help people take more control over their behavior and personality traits, considering they are more in touch with why they act the way they do.

Takeaways:

- Sometimes the best way to discover something about ourselves to is to ask seemingly innocent questions, then read between the lines. The way we answer these types of questions can be more honest and indicative than intentionally trying to figure out your personality and identity.
- The first way to do this is through the seven stories exercise, which implores you to find your seven greatest accomplishments and write the stories involved in those triumphs. What comes out in the story will tell you more about

who you are and what you seek than trying to answer those questions alone.
- The second method to discover yourself is through Carl Jung's personality test, which consists of four questions: name a color, name an animal, name a body of water, and think about a white room. The ensuing adjectives you use to describe each of those answers will tell you something specific about your personality that your psyche may not consciously have realized.

Chapter 7. Self-Awareness Questions

Famous Greek philosopher Aristotle (384–322 BC) stated, "Knowing yourself is the beginning of all wisdom," and founding father of the United States of America Benjamin Franklin couldn't have said it better: "There are three things extremely hard: steel, a diamond, and to know one's self." The comparison of self-awareness to that of other "invincible" things factors just how important it was to philosophers in history.

Self-awareness is one of the most sought-after feelings of human existence. Everyone wants to be sure of themselves and know who they are what they represent. It's not that we are happier with that knowledge—the knowledge itself is neutral. But it's what that knowledge represents that makes us want it.

When we are self-aware, we feel that we are living our best selves, correcting our errors, and seizing our full potential. One of those is probably the reason you picked up this book in the first place. Psychologists and scientists also believe in the need for self-awareness. They view this consciousness as a direct relation to some of the most essential states of being. These states of being are greater happiness, less inner conflict, and more confidence in decision-making.

Greater Happiness

Happiness is not a physical thing that can be defined. Every person has his or her own version of what happiness looks or feels like. But regardless of what it is to each person, the act of achieving it comes from being more self-aware because you know what you want.

People are able to express themselves more freely without judgment.

Happiness can look very different to everyone, so understanding oneself allows them to find his or her own version. You may have been following someone else's blueprint or template, but the second you find your own is a moment of triumph.

Less Inner Conflict

When people act upon their inner feelings and values, there may be times when they feel some type of inner conflict with themselves. With a more heightened sense of self, it becomes less likely that inner feelings and outside actions will ever collide. This is especially felt in making decisions.

Regardless of the type of decisions being made—buying a sweater or choosing a life partner—it can almost be guaranteed that decision-making will be that much easier with a stronger, self-aware individual. People will have set personal guidelines they can apply to solve everyday problems and thus make better choices.

So how do we actually gain self-awareness? The focus is geared around having people ask themselves simple and direct questions that hopefully hint at things just outside our conscious knowledge.

Typically, people will analyze and reflect on their nature versus nurture upbringing, environments, and social circles to gather their sense of self. They'll ask themselves questions, again, such as "What makes me happy and fulfilled?" This should be considered a mediocre starting point, because the only type of answer you are going to construct from this is a lovely-sounding platitude that doesn't actually give you insight into yourself.

And so, this chapter works to provide a simpler way of achieving self-awareness. No one knows you better than yourself, and sometimes, that's the problem with gaining self-awareness. You may not lie to yourself, but you are privy to all of your own thoughts, whereas others can only observe your actual actions and behaviors—which are what really represent who you are in the world.

Remember, the actual answers to these questions are not the important part. These questions are phrased as they are to challenge and inspire deep thought. They ask people to dive deeper into understanding why they answered the way they did and dig into their behavioral and thought patterns.

1. What kind of prize would I work hardest for, or what punishment would I work hardest to avoid?

The answer to this question might help identify the true motive behind an individual's drive. Beyond surface-level things, what is really motivating people? Is this something they care about? And what type of pain or pleasure matters to them? On an instinctual level, what really matters the most in both a positive and negative way?

Gamblers all want one prize: the jackpot. They try and try again, whether it be scratchers or slot machines to try and win that big prize money. Is there hope is that they will eventually win back all of the money they've already spent into their gambling habit? Is their hope to become richer than they can imagine?

Why are they working so hard? You might discover that their motivation is the thrill and rush of the risk involved. Do they care about making steady pay or finding their purpose? Perhaps not. When you can dig into what someone wants the most and why, you can often find what is driving them without having to ask it directly.

2. Where do you want to spend money, and where are you fine going cheap or skipping altogether?

This answer may reveal what matters to someone's daily living and what they want to experience or avoid in their lives. There comes a point where material belongings no longer have a meaning or purpose for someone. For example, sometimes, spending money on experiences instead of a new purse has the potential to improve someone's overall well-being and outlook on life.

What do you have no problem splurging on, and what doesn't matter to you? When deciding on vacation finances, people may opt to splurge on a boat trip and stay in a shabby hotel. This reveals their desire to experience an unforgettable moment rather than staying in a nice hotel, what they view as a waste of money. Others might opt for the opposite and revel in their creature comforts while not seeing much of the scenery. In either case, they've used their money to quite literally identify and spend their priorities.

Where your money goes is an important part of what makes you happy, so if you can pay attention to where you let it flow and where you cut it off, you'll immediately know what matters to you on a daily basis.

3. What is your most personally significant and meaningful achievement and also your most meaningful disappointment or failure?

It is pretty common that experiences, whether they're good or bad, shape people into who they are for the present and future. Significant experiences also tend to create their self-identities—*you are this kind of person because you did this and succeeded or failed*. Achievements and failures tie into how someone sees oneself. Overall, it's about how people want to see themselves.

This question will get a response about how people view themselves, good or bad. Failure will evoke flaws they hate, while achievements will bring up to strengths they are proud of.

A career woman who has worked her way up the corporate ladder might reflect on her accomplishment. She looks back to the things she did in order to get that corner office. She discovers that her resilience and determination helped her push through obstacles to get to where she is now. The story about her career accomplishments is actually a story about the positive traits she utilized in reaching that point—her self-identity. You can imagine the same negative type of self-identity might unfold if the same woman were to talk about her failures.

The way that people answer this question shows that they can identify positive and negative experiences and dissect why they hold particular values either so high or low.

4. What is effortless and what is always exhausting?

This is a question that is designed to tell you where you should spend your time. Some people are better at things than others. Engineers are great at math while artists are masters of creativity. Lawyers are great at arguing a point while teachers do best at inspiring young minds. What might people say about you?

Whatever aspects of life, occupation notwithstanding, come easily and naturally to you are things you should emphasize and capitalize on. The things that are always challenging and exhausting may be worthwhile, but they may also be things you should simply let go of. The way people answer this question should help them tap into their best strengths and areas for improvement.

For instance, as a baker answers this question, she may automatically recognize her creative niche for blending ingredients together to make a beautiful dessert. She will see that although she has practiced perfecting her craft, it has naturally been very easy for as long as she can remember. She just sees outside the box in a way that few other bakers can.

On the other hand, it may take her much longer to write and follow traditional recipes. As she reflects on these natural strengths and weaknesses, she can look at herself and design a career that better suits her strengths and weaknesses instead of trying to conform to other people. This is all because she recognized her natural talents and followed them.

5. If you could design a character in a game, what traits would you emphasize and which would you ignore?

Similar to Question 5, this helps people focus on their ideal selves. Imagine that you have a limited amount of points to give a person but six traits to spread the points across. Which will you choose to emphasize and bolster, and which will you choose to leave average or even lacking? It's more than likely that this either represents how you see yourself or how you would like to see yourself. You might even create someone entirely different from who you are.

For someone answering this question, it helps them identify what they consider to be their strengths and flaws. The strengths you can continue to make front and center, while the weaknesses can be pinpointed to be worked on.

6. What charity would you donate millions to if you had to?

Besides reflecting on the needs of oneself, there now comes the test of someone's worldwide view. Asking this question forces one to think about the values and needs of others and what they care about outside of themselves.

Will you donate to an animal shelter or a charity for cancer? Perhaps you would sponsor a child from a third-world country? They all say very different things about you. Whatever the case, it tells you how you want to see the world and what types of causes matter to you.

Being able to ask these questions evokes a deeper connection to one's own values, ideas, and awareness. They influence people to take a step back, think, and wholeheartedly answer questions not typical of finding their identities. Afterward, the hope is that there is some type of action plan component following acknowledgment of their traits and behavior patterns.

The purpose of asking these is to, again, examine behavior. Plus, it helps people see what their personalities and identities are all about. There is a wide range of information that can be discovered through these questions rather than just being a delivery of information itself.

These questions are much more heartfelt and guide a person in thinking about the most relevant aspects of his or her character. These questions make people think beyond predictable statements that organically stimulate more meaningful thought. Then more influence is placed on creating some type of objective to achieve.

When it comes to particular questions, it's good to figure out a plan for achieving next steps and making applicable changes. The questions help to influence and motivate. The person who answers these questions will then capitalize on their revelations and put the plan into action, so to speak.

Then it's also important to remember that it's not only the actual answers that help someone identify their own awareness of himself. The point is to look beyond the answers and read between the lines. Critical thinking, evaluation, and reflection are the key skills at play here.

People must critically analyze their answers and where those answers came from. From there, they need to apply this newfound sense of awareness to further enhance their own quality of life. Where are things going well and what can be improved? Further, how might one get started with applying their realizations as catalysts for change?

Overall, the ideal is to improve happiness while eliminating things that make them unhappy. Being self-aware and understanding one's own identity is one of the most important steps toward reaching true happiness.

Remember that happiness is only measurable by each individual. Although happiness comes in different shapes and forms for people, the act of achieving it can be the same for every person who uses these questions to guide them on the right path. The road to happiness is about discovering oneself and learning to formulate a scheme in reaching and sustaining that happiness.

Takeaways:

- Self-awareness is important, but not easily gained. That's why it's so highly valued.
- The best way to gain self-awareness is to ask about your behaviors and actions, not your intentions or thoughts. Your thoughts are too easily corrupted or otherwise simply not representative of what you actually feel. When you can analyze your behaviors and actions, you can then glean real information about yourself.

Chapter 8. Effecting Change

We've covered quite a bit of information and research regarding personality and identity thus far. Though there may not be a consensus on all of it, one thing is sure: people all have good and bad aspects of their character. There are things that people want to maintain and things they'd like to change completely about themselves.

Sometimes, people come to a realization that who they are in certain areas of their lives are not who or where they want to be. They might even reach this realization from this book. So they want to make a positive change.

Just like with any major change, it's something that doesn't happen overnight. Personality is something that is formed over time, similar to the development of habits. As you may know, habits can be hard not only to break, but also to reinforce. There are processes involved in wanting to change one's personality, but most importantly, there needs to be a willingness for change.

It's important to understand why a change or improvement in personality matters in the first place. The reason change may matter to you is because we are all subject to people's judgments every day. The whole concept of judging a book by its cover really rings true here. It doesn't even matter if people are correct about you; they'll judge what they see, and this can last the duration of your relationship. This can work for you or against you.

In a study listed in the *European Journal of Personality* (2011), about 60 participants were asked to wear particular shirts that carried a specific smell. Following the experiment, it was concluded that people are able to distinguish someone's personality based on the smell of the T-shirt. Of all personality traits, the top three that were easy to spot were neuroticism, extraversion, and dominance.

Another study conducted by Stowinski for the *Journal of The Royal Society Interface* (2016) revealed that the way people moved could be strong revealers of their personalities to others. Research from this study showed that people have particular "individual motor signatures" that made it easy for others to see and make a judgment from there. These can also be considered to be certain mannerisms that people have when interacting with others.

Why do these studies matter in this context? People were able to make a pretty educated guess as to how someone would be without even knowing them—only by watching how they moved or by smelling their scent. Simply by looking at a few features, people were able to dissect one another without even needing to talk to or know a person.

Again, this can work for you or against you. Being more aware of this can help people represent their personality traits in ways they want to be represented.

The Desire for Happiness

As people begin their paths toward making positive changes in their personality traits, it's also important to understand what they should be aiming toward. There is a general desire for increased happiness and fulfillment, but what set of personality traits does that contain? Just what are the traits of happy personalities? This may look slightly different for everyone, but there are actually proven traits that correlate extremely highly with happiness and well-being. If nothing else, it's just a good guideline to aim toward.

In particular, there are 11 dimensions of well-being that have been studied based on three primary models of well-being: subjective well-being, psychological well-being, and PERMA. Traditionally, people associate smiling and positive vibes as indicators of happy people. In more modern research, it's been shown that multiple well-being aspects go far beyond these typical observations. Notably, the vast majority of these are controllable the vast majority of the time. In other words, it's up to you.

1. High Positive Emotions. This trait exhibits someone who has a very high frequency and intensity when it comes to positive emotions and moods.

2. Low Negative Emotions. In conjunction with #1, this trait allows a person to have a low frequency and intensity of negative emotions and moods.

3. Life Satisfaction. When evaluating oneself, it can be determined this type of person is one who has a subjective yet positive outlook. He or she will consider any information to be relevant and take it with a grain of salt. This can also be known as being rational and reasonable.

4. Autonomy. Independence is key when it comes to this trait. One is not pressured by societal expectations.

5. Environmental Mastery. When one feels there's a need to shape his or her environment to fit his or her needs, it happens seamlessly with this trait. These people observe their surroundings and can easily adjust themselves to fit in that environment.

6. Personal Growth. Instead of reaching a sense of learning plateaus, one is always wanting to grow, improve and learn more about oneself.

7. Positive Relations. The types of relationships that someone with this trait are those that are warm and interpersonal.

8. Self-Acceptance. There is no criticism for someone who maintains a positive attitude about oneself.

9. Purpose and Meaning in Life. For someone with this trait, he or she is confident in his or her life path and efforts in life choices. These people understand that there is a connection to greater things than themselves.

10. Engagement in Life. Outside of daily responsibilities, these people have true engagement and interest in their lives. They have a desire to get the most meaning out of their lives while being fully vested in everything they do or encounter.

11. Accomplishment. People who set goals and work toward achieving them are those with the accomplishment trait. Once they achieve these goals, they have a sense of mastery and efficacy.

A study conducted by Jessie Sun, Luke Smillie, and Scott Berry Kaufman of over 700 participants called "Unique Associations Between Big Five Personality Aspects and Multiple Dimensions of Well-Being" analyzed the connection between well-being's multiple aspects and a wide variety of personality dispositions. They came up with five additional personality traits that were fundamental to increased happiness.

1. Enthusiasm. Those who are enthusiastic are very friendly, expressive, and sociable. Enthusiastic people such as motivational speakers tend to give off very energetic and positive vibes in any environment.

2. Low Withdrawal. These types of people do not get discouraged and overwhelmed. A teacher with low withdrawal wouldn't take it personally if a student sleeps during a class period. Instead, this teacher would make an effort to either change up the lesson or speak with the student privately afterward.

3. Industriousness. People with this trait are achievement-oriented, efficient, and have high work ethics. Entrepreneurs are a prime example of these types of people. Their high aspirations and ways of meeting those goals are always what sets them apart from their counterparts.

4. Compassion. To be compassionate means that these people are aware and considerate of other people's feelings and emotions. Humanitarians and volunteers are truly compassionate people, as they selflessly give their time to help others in need.

5. Intellectual Curiosity. Being open and wanting to learn are just some of the characteristics of this trait. These people will do a lot of reflection and deep thinking to help themselves grow in any situation. Even as adults, learning is constant and there is always a drive to learn more.

These studies and findings prove that there are many paths that one can take to achieve positive well-being. Well-being has to do with extraversion and emotional stability. Individuals have the capacity to make changes in their personalities in order to achieve their true happiness.

Through their own influence in thinking, emotions, and behaviors, it's highly possible for them to make positive impacts on their own growth and personalities. As they become more aware and empowered by their ability to change their personalities, they can be happier with themselves.

Achieving Change

When it comes to changing one's personality, it is evident that there are real benefits behind doing so. People can do it and have been doing it. There's been some great research to also prove that in making these changes, people experienced more happiness and contentment with their life choices.

Research from Dr. Lesley Sue Martin (University of Wollongong, Australia) revealed that people who were motivated enough to change their personalities could do so in just about 10 weeks' time. With the right combination of *motivation and coaching*, this type of change was greatly achievable. All it took was some guidance and a willingness to learn.

You probably have your own motivations, so let the rest of this chapter be the guidance to put you over the edge. One might ask, "How do I change and adapt my personality traits?" Just like with behavior, it comes down to mastering the art of gaining or eliminating habits. It helps to start with incremental changes that will eventually lead to bigger and more impactful ones.

Go into Different Environments

Changing a personality can occur when there is a new life experience. Those who underwent severe emotional trauma or experienced some form of life-changing event have a tendency to make significant changes to their personalities as well. There are even times where a social role has influence over how someone changes his or her personality.

People who become parents or those who are placed in high-ranking job positions may suddenly realize that they must be much more conscientious of themselves and people around them. Their newfound responsibilities will force them to change things, such as how they think, feel, and behave, especially around others.

New relationships can spark changes in people as they learn to be more open to their significant other's perspectives and they have to be more mindful about someone else's emotions. If the man is accustomed to being harmlessly flirtatious with other women, it may cause a rift in his relationship with his girlfriend. She can feel disrespected and unappreciated. From here, he will need to understand her feelings and stop his behavior if he wants the relationship to work. Initially, it may seem like he's making a sacrifice, but he'll soon learn that these changes made him into a more caring and respectful partner.

The more that people go through in their lives, the more chances they will get to change their personalities, naturally. If you want to change your personality traits, put yourself into environments or even roles where you will be forced to do so. It's unlikely that you'll create change by going through your same routines.

Do the Change. Don't Think It.

All ideas are great, but they are nothing without implementation. Taking action is the only thing that will really matter at the end of the day, as it becomes the bottom line. People shouldn't fool themselves into thinking that the ideas themselves will help make any difference in their lives. It takes a real action plan to put those ideas into motion.

The first steps are always the scariest, but taking action is a move in the right direction. It'll make people uncomfortable and they will feel like they're jumping into the deep end of a pool. However, without trial by fire, people will ever know what the outcome is.

An overweight man trying to lose 50 pounds to save his life may experience multiple struggles along his journey. He may get discouraged by seeing other healthy people as well as the frustration of not losing weight as fast as he'd like. After all, he became overweight because of compulsive behavior and lack of self-control.

He needs to be the trait that he's wanting to achieve—self-controlled and disciplined. He can't simply keep thinking about it and pining for it. If he's able to stay on the path toward real change, he's able to improve his health and success. First, he'll need to identify his triggers for compulsiveness and adjust when needed. As he begins to make these small yet impactful changes, it will help him continue to stay on track with his eye on the final prize—health and weight loss. As long as he steers the course, he will see success and inner happiness.

Setting Goals.

It's been proven that when people are more specific about the steps they take toward accomplishing their goals, they are that much more likely to achieve those goals.

Essentially, having a plan is what makes goal achievement much more feasible. Instead of someone saying that they'll make three new friends, they should instead set the following goals: attend four separate parties or networking events. Then they should talk to at least 10 different people at each of those events, leaving with some contact information. Plus, they should also have made plans to meet with at least one of those individuals.

Having concrete plans rather than those that are more abstract make it much easier to define and achieve specific milestones.

Think about someone wanting to improve his stage presence when performing. First, he'd need to be able to identify what he wants to change. If it's adding more charisma, then he'll need to study others as well as practice it himself. To see more definitive results of his journey, he should set incremental goals that will not only help him gain more confidence on stage but at the same time perfect his craft through mentors and work experience.

There are multiple facets to being a great performer who displays charisma. This performer should be mindful of his steps toward achieving his desired trait. A small yet monumental step would be going to watching videos of people seamlessly engaging with the crowds. Then he should attempt to mimic those traits and watch the experience snowball from there. Eventually, he'll become much more positive and validated with each small goal he accomplishes as he gets better with each show.

Understanding Motivations.

It's important to not think about the tough task at hand. Instead, think about what really matters in the end. In essence, look at the bigger picture. There's always going to be a pleasure or benefit that people are seeking, as well as a pain or discomfort they are avoiding.

One of the first steps toward changing one's life is being clear about how this change will happen. Then there needs to be an understanding of what will be left behind as well as everything to look forward to. In many cases, sacrifices will need to be made in order to achieve the bigger goals. For people trying to pay off a large amount of credit card debt, they have to sacrifice going out to eat or sticking within a strict budget to really make a dent in paying off debt. The motivations have to be crystal clear and tangible; otherwise, the sacrifices won't seem worthwhile.

A recovering addict is someone who must mindfully and purposefully, every day, spend time remaining sober. He must follow all steps in his recovery program to make a positive change in his life. From a personality standpoint, he must focus on leaving behind his addictive behavior.

The thing that keeps him going is sobriety and a clear life ahead, drug-free. The motivation behind his efforts is being able to live a conscious and fulfilling life that was once hazed by the emptiness of drug use. That seems like something worth sacrificing for. Once he is able to rid himself of his addictive tendencies, he's able to find more meaning in living life with purpose.

Change the Narrative.

Sometimes, the best person to get through to an individual is himself. People have the tendency to create self-fulfilling prophecies for themselves but don't end up changing because they tell themselves they can't do it. So in order to change that, the narrative has to change.

People have to reinvent the picture they have of themselves. With the simple change of perspective, they change how they see themselves and how they represent themselves to others. Reflection is a key component when it comes to self-awareness.

Change is able to occur when the individual believes in him or herself. Without any change in the story, everything leading up to it will seem almost pointless. Once people tell themselves who they are long enough, they will begin to believe it.

Many people who have a fear of public speaking will avoid it at all costs. They lack the confidence in themselves and what they are able to present to others. But with consistent self-talk and changing their narrative to boost their confidence, they would be able to walk out to a crowd and speak without feeling nervous and anxious. They will talk themselves through the situation and come to the realization that it's not as bad as it always seems. In fact, they'll come to realize that it's actually fun and inspiring.

Change is a wonderful thing. Whether it be through self-affirmations or setting specific goals, it's important for people to always find ways to reflect and evaluate every aspect of their lives. If it's possible to make changes for the better, then by all means, those opportunities should be grasped.

Takeaways:

- Creating a change in your personality and identity is not as difficult as you may think. It is, however, perhaps more important than you might think. It can simultaneously make you feel happier and more fulfilled while also avoiding malicious judgment from others.
- In fact, there have been 16 interrelated personality traits associated with well-being and happiness. It wouldn't do them justice to list them all out here, but it's a helpful guideline of what you can or should be changing.
- One of the ways to effectuate change is to change your environment and see the personality change as an adaptation. You can also focus on doing the change and not thinking about it, understanding motivations, setting clearer goals, and changing your self-narrative.

Chapter 9. Personality Potpourri

The focus of this chapter is going to be some of the smaller aspects of personality and identity. These are notable and interesting aspects of identity that haven't necessarily been introduced or covered anywhere else. All are different in their own right but have to do with ways that people discover their personalities and identities.

One thing they all do have in common is that they provide a different perspective and insight into the understanding of personality and identity. Researchers, scientists, theorists, and general people all have their opinions as to where personalities come from. It's worth exploring some of these other unique and fascinating studies.

Type A vs. Type B

When talking about personality types, some of the most common forms is that of two types: A and B. Can someone's personality affect his or her health? This particular question has been the subject of decades of research.

Ray Rosenman and Meyer Friedman conducted research that studied the relationship between personality, stress, and health since the 1950s. This also led to a published text in 1974 entitled *Type A Behavior and Your Heart.*

Both Rosenman and Friedman began observing the seats in their patient waiting rooms. They noticed that some of the seats were much more significantly worn than others. Plus, they also saw that some of the worn areas of the seats were not really in typical areas. The fronts of the seats were worn and this suggested that more fidgety patients would occupy those ones.

The doctors noticed that the fidgety patients were anxious as they waited for their appointment. They would stand and sit more than other patients, causing the fronts to be worn. The cardiologists concluded that these patients could be categorized as having Type A personality traits.

Usually, Type A personalities would be described as those who are a bit on the perfectionist, aggressive, and anxious side. They like things to be done a certain way, in a certain time, and they are highly organized. Type B personalities, on the other hand, are more peaceful and centered in their evaluation of life's events, and they tend to not sweat the small stuff.

Those with Type A personalities are considered more prone to experiencing stress. They are typically impatient and anxious in stressful situations. When put under pressure, their tension levels rise much easier than other people. On the contrary, those with Type B personality traits differ in how they handle stressful situations. Type B personalities tend to be less affected and can let go of worries easier than a Type A.

When people deal with high levels of stress, this can easily lead to increased health risks as well. In a dynamic and continuous study, Friedman and Rosenman were able to conclude that patients with Type A behaviors were more likely to suffer from coronary heart diseases, also known as CHD. They found that these individuals' risk factors for health complications were much higher than the rest of the samples studied.

Furthermore, both Friedman and Rosenman wanted to emphasize that the effects of Type A personalities were associated with "behavioral patterns." So this meant that it wasn't considered to be directly determined by an individual's personality. Friedman and Rosenman offered suggestions on how people with Type A personalities would be able to alter their behavior when responding to stressful situations.

Normally, it's pretty common for people to say that Type A personalities are those who are very organized and prepared. However, there comes a time where a lot of that organization and preparedness are exhausted at extreme levels, making a person stressed and overwhelmed. This is when it can lead to more health-related issues.

Now, take a typical Type A personality individual such as a party planner. She is always stressed because she must plan out everything perfectly before a big event to impress clients and audiences. She maps out all of the decor details and calls all vendors to confirm appointments. With this pressure, she tends to be very high strung, rude, and anxious until the event is over. She isn't happy until the end product is complete, where she will then start her negative stress cycle all over again for another event.

According to Friedman and Rosenman, this same woman can change her levels of happiness by adjusting to exhibit more Type B personality traits than Type A. This meant that she had the ability to control her own personality and how she was going to react in certain situations—being more relaxed than high-strung. Instead of lashing out a worker for the event, she could take a few breaths and try to evaluate the situation. When problem-solving, she could utilize the assistance of others around her to help ease her own responsibilities and pressures. The delegation of duties can help her focus on other priorities, thus helping her relax and be more Type B.

Being able to change one's personality based on stressful situations and how he or she reacts to them is a great way to improve one's overall health and well-being. Understanding that there is an alternative to reacting in certain situations in a more productive and positive outlook is a great first step for someone trying to channel more Type B traits over Type A ones.

Transactional Analysis

This is another concept that focuses on communication habits as a form of identifying one's personality. Sometimes, people can also change their personalities based on who they are speaking with at the moment. In particular, this theory is known as transactional analysis—developed by Eric Berne in 1960.

Transactional analysis, or TA, is where every person has a total of three different aspects associated with their personalities—the Parent, the Adult and the Child. Depending on who they are speaking with, every person will take on a different role.

Transactional analysis is empowering for people in controlling and changing their own personalities. With it, they have the ability to identify their roles when communicating with other people. They can adjust accordingly, which would mean that they can also affect the outcome of any conflict in communication as long as they recognize their roles.

The Parent. This role consists of being in charge and telling others what to do. At some point in their lives, they were told what to do from people in authority like parents, teachers, and government. From these experiences, they absorbed those authoritative traits and exhibit them to other people, depending on who they're talking to. Parents are usually ones that always have to be the rule-maker and enforcer.

The Adult. This role consists of reasoned judgment. They are careful and considerate in planning and making sure things go off without a hitch. Even though Adults can exhibit Parent traits, they are different because their motivation is reason versus authority.

The Child. The last role consists of purely emotional thoughts and behaviors. This can be in the form of emotions like anger and humor. A Child will likely not reason or come to an understanding. Everything has to do with emotion rather than finding practical reasons.

All three of these aspects identify how people are when they are communicating with one another. In terms of communication, two people participate in what's considered to be a *transaction*. If people experience problems, it's because their transactions with others were deemed to be unsuccessful.

Typically, Parents speak to their children in roles of being a parent. They may also speak with other Parents and Adults, and usually, their subject matter may also be about their children. There are also different types of Parents and how they communicate with their children. More often than not, these aspects of their personalities are evoked by the opposite.

Communication can be easy in some instances and much more complex in others. How can people determine which situations will be easier for them to handle over another? Well, there are two common types of transactions that people will encounter that will test their abilities to communicate effectively.

People who are at the same social level are those who will most like experience *complementary* transactions. Normally, this will be communication occurring being a Parent and another Parent. Both people will often have similar ways of thinking and this makes communication easier between the two.

On the other hand, conflicts will usually occur during *crossed* transactions. This is where two people are of different levels such as Parent to Child. Since their thinking process and maturity levels differ, it makes it that much more likely that conflict will occur. They hardly agree on anything as each person has a completely different perspective than the other.

Whether the Parent is nurturing or controlling, he or she is still speaking to a Child. This Child can either be adaptive or natural with his or her response. When both parties are talking to each other with one being the Parent and the other being the Child, their wires get crossed along the way and conflict will arise.

It's clear that the ideal line of communication is one that comes from a mature and rational Adult to Adult relationship. Peers or colleagues who work well with each other will typically fall into this positive relationship. In order to have rational conversations over conflicting ones, it's important that people move themselves and others to the Adult level.

For instance, two adults in a romantic relationship will respect one another's values, ways of thinking, and choices they make in their lives. Since both parties have similar thinking, maturity, and consideration for each other's well-being, it makes it easier for them to communicate. They set expectations with one another and understand each other's needs in the relationship.

Lack of communication usually occurs between people of different roles. A controlling Parent will typically evoke an adaptive Child, also known as a naughty child. The Parent who always needs to hover over the Child can make the child rebellious and lash out, working counterproductively against the parent. Then, as the Child grows up, he or she can take on a role of opposing Parent or Adult states.

Again, the ideal is to have a balanced and rational Adult to Adult relationship. Even if people feel like they cannot control how another person communicates with them, they can try to take on the mature role and evoke the other person to do the same. This will, in turn, reduce levels of conflict that may occur in communication.

Gender and Personality

Everyone has most likely heard the coined phrase that "men are from Mars and women are from Venus." So it comes as no surprise that there are going to be significant gender differences when it comes to personalities. We can talk about stereotypes all we want about this, but it's more convincing to go straight to what science has shown us.

Italian cognitive psychologist Marco Del Giudice studied the comparison of men's and women's personality traits. He sampled over 10,000 people and was able to discover major differences between the two genders.

Women would score much higher than men in traits such as:
- Sensitivity
- Warmth
- Apprehension

Men would score higher than their counterparts in:
- Emotional stability
- Dominance
- Rule-consciousness
- Vigilance

Overall, the study suggests that personality-wise, men and women belong on completely different sides of the species spectrum. In this way, we can see where stereotypes form rather than applying them to people without understanding their basis.

Women tend to be more nurturing and understanding of others. They will be more reasonable and empathetic to others. Men, however, might be more stern and vigilant. When deciding on punishment or consequences for their child, a mother might be more warming while the father is demanding and strict. The mother might also be apprehensive in coming up with an appropriate consequence and the father is quick to make a fair and rational judgment.

Another study by researchers Paul Costa and Robert McCrae in 2001 studied over 23,000 men and women across 26 different cultures. They attempted to graph the difference in male and female personality by utilizing the Big Five factor traits. Cultural diversity ranged from people from the United States, Hong Kong, Russia, and India.

Participants were to fill out personality questionnaires. Women would rate themselves as being friendly, warm, anxious, and sensitive. Meanwhile, men would rate themselves as being assertive and open to any new ideas. Both genders believed they exhibited these traits more than each other.

The study also showed that women scored higher in agreeableness and neuroticism as well as one facet of openness to experience. In simple terms, this meant that they were more pleasing, high-strung, and willing. The men scored higher in one facet of extraversion and a different facet of openness to experience than the women.

In social situations, women might tend to feel out the environment and people before she begins to make conversation with people. She might also be more conforming in her communication with others for the sake of keeping conversations neutral and conflict-free. A man in this same situation might be more domineering and more extroverted.

Although both genders scored one facet of openness to experience, they both have different perspectives and feelings about what they are open to. Women can be more open to trying out new hobbies when men are more apt to trying out new restaurants.

So why are genders so different in personalities? For one, it could be that it's biological and that men and women are just wired differently. It has been shown that men's brains function differently than those of women. Studies show that men have a harder time with multitasking, which could help explain why women get upset with them for having so-called selective hearing. Men really could just be having a hard time processing what's being said while they're trying to do something else.

It could also have to do with socialization and what each gender roles play in society. Reinforcements can happen simply from interactions between men and women. Due to either positive or negative stigma in society for gender roles, some people just acclimate themselves into those roles because that's what they see every day. Women might be more caring for others and men have to prove themselves as being "men" by being tough.

Another factor could be survival mechanisms. Females would fare most in having offspring, thus initiating their innate survival skills. As mothers, especially, women automatically have a protective and strong role in their personalities. Like a mama bear, they're not letting anyone harm their child and they're also willing to do anything to ensure its survival. Men also have these protective instincts but theirs might stem from competing with others to express more of a male dominance.

The Enneagram

Although there are many tests that people can use to discover their personality types, one, in particular, is very interesting and enlightening. The Enneagram test was developed in the 1960s as a way for people to attain *self-actualization*. The focus is primarily on self-improvement because it forces people to face their own faults head on. What makes it unique is that it aims to identify the *how* and *why* rather than the *what* people do. Rather than dive into the minutiae, it's helpful to have a broad overview of the types of possible outcomes form the Enneagram and try to spot yourself in them.

There are nine types that can be identified when taking this test.

Type One—The Reformer. These types of people are usually concerned with always being right and have a high level of integrity. They can also be deemed as being judgmental and self-righteous. Examples include priests and doctors.

Type Two—The Helper. These people have a yearning to be loved and appreciated. They are usually very generous but can also be seen as manipulative and prideful. Examples include mothers and teachers.

Type Three—The Achiever. These types of people love to be praised and applauded. They are workaholics, which can make them narcissistic and vain. Examples include actors and students.

Type Four—The Individualist. Typically, these types will search for meaning in their lives with a need to be unique. They are certainly creative but can also be moody and temperamental. Examples include musicians and painters.

Type Five—The Investigator. These people strive to be knowledgeable and competent. Most of the time, they are very objective but they have the tendency to hoard themselves away. An example includes researchers.

Type Six—The Loyalist. These people are thoughtful in their planning and are very loyal to anyone they care about. They do question everything and this can make them suspicious and paranoid. Examples include survivalists and police officers.

Type Seven—The Enthusiast. These types of people like adventure and are very energetic. They make the best of everything and this can force them to be reckless and overindulgent. Examples include thrill-seekers and actors.

Type Eight—The Challenger. These people always have to be in control or power. They are assertive, which can come off as being aggressive and extreme. Examples include overbearing parents or people in the military.

Type Nine—The Peacemaker. Lastly, these people are stable and mediate situations. They're normally easygoing and accepting of all things. But this type of naive behavior can make them oblivious to negative things happening around them. Examples include hippies and grandparents

Some people may exhibit a bit of each of these types or be more dominant in just a few. Taking the test allows people to gain a better understanding of themselves and why they act the way they do in certain situations. The test forces people to look at themselves in a deeper way that could potentially unlock unconscious ways of thinking.

Again, we circle back to the underlying question of why self-discovery is so important.

For one, it helps people understand that they might want to skew more toward a Type B existence for their own good.

Second, if they are able to recognize their roles when they communicate with other people, they can better gauge and appropriate their personalities and transactions with others effectively.

Third, simply understanding the differences between gender personalities helps people become more aware of their own traits.

People all have different personalities and identities. The beauty of life comes from the way that people interact with one another based on their own acknowledgment or subconscious exhibition of their traits. Having a little better understanding as to where those traits come from and how people display those traits is something that will help them grow and become more aware of their own identities.

Takeaways:

- We are all familiar with the concept of Type A and Type B personalities, but were you aware that there is certainly one type that will allow you to live longer and more happily? It's the type which lets you approach life from a less anxious lens: Type B.
- Transactional analysis is a theory of communication and roles. There are three possible roles for us to take in any interaction, and which role we take depends on the other person: Parent, Adult, or Child. You may have noticed

similar patterns in your own life where you felt you had to take charge (or the opposite) with specific people.
- Genders have different personalities, and though it begrudges me to say this, many of the differences you can already imagine due to intense gender stereotyping. Additionally, everything about a gender you think would be tied to an evolutionary basis also shows correlation.
- The Enneagram test is the final personality and identity test we cover in this book. It is composed of nine general types of personalities: reformer, helper, achiever, individualist, investigator, loyalist, enthusiast, challenger, and peacemaker.

Summary Guide

Chapter 1. The Origins of Identity and Personality

- The study of personality and identity has been a compelling issue for as long as we have been sentient beings. Like many disciplines, study seemed to have begun in ancient Greece with the theory of humorism—where four separate bodily fluids were present in the body in varying quantities that gave rise to different personalities and four temperaments in particular.
- One of the most seminal personality theories was put forth by Sigmund Freud hundreds of years later. This is known as the structural model, and you know it by its three components: the id, ego, and superego. Like the humors, they worked together in varying amounts to form a unique personality. The id is a hedonist,

the ego is the mediator, while the superego is the conscience.
- There is a strong biological basis for differences in personality. First, intrasexual and intersexual traits have formed the baseline for our modern personalities in many ways. Second, there are literal biological and physical differences between those who score differently on the Big Five personality traits.
- Why does this all matter? It's simple, actually. If you don't know where you are coming from and where you are right now, how are you supposed to know where you should go next?

Chapter 2. The Big Five Personality Traits

- The Big Five personality traits are one of the first attempts to classify people based on specific traits rather than as a whole. You can remember the traits easily with the acronym OCEAN: openness to experience (trying new things), conscientiousness (being cautious and careful), extroversion (drawing energy from others and social situations), agreeableness (warm and sympathetic), and neuroticism (anxious and high-strung).

- Unlike other assessments in this book, there have actually been determined to be a winning formula for these traits—not per se, but if you display certain traits, you are more likely to have better mental health and increased happiness. If you are more of the first four traits (OCEA) and less neurotic, you will tend to be happier and more fulfilled in life. It's not hard to understand why—you'll have more experiences, you'll live longer from your caution, you'll have a wider social circle and support system, you'll get along better with others, and you'll be less anxious and more relaxed.

Chapter 3. Myers, Briggs, and Keirsey

- The MBTI, though helpful as a guideline, can sometimes suffer from people treating it like a horoscope and reading into their type what they wish to see about themselves.

- The MBTI functions on four distinct traits and how much of each trait you are or are not. The traits are generally introverted/extroverted (your general attitude toward others), intuitive/feeling (how you perceive information), thinking/feeling (how you process information), and perceiving/judging (how you implement information). Thus, this creates 16 distinct personality types.
- The MBTI does suffer from some shortcomings, including the lack of subtlety when most people are a bit of each trait, the usage of stereotyping to classify people, and the lack of consistency when people score differently depending on their current moods and circumstances.
- The Keirsey temperaments were a way of organizing the same information gleaned from the MBTI. Here, there are four distinct temperaments, each with two types of roles, instead of 16 personality types. The four temperaments are guardian, artisan, idealistic, and rational. Keirsey himself estimated that up to 80%

of the population fell into the first two temperaments.

Chapter 4. Unconscious Upbringings

- An interesting subset of personality science is the ways people theorize we are influenced by our upbringings. Since this is largely while we were young children, this is said to be mostly unconscious and instinctual according to our early experiences.
- One theory is Adler's birth order theory, which states that the interaction between the first, middle, and youngest children in a family and how they compete for the affection and attention of the parents creates personality traits by themselves.
- The other prevailing theory on unconscious upbringings is attachment theory by Bowlby, which states that the way we view relationships with others is a direct result of how safe and secure we feel in regards to our caretakers as children. If you felt secure, you likely have secure attachment as an adult. If you felt less than secure, you could have any of

the other three types of attachment: anxious-preoccupied, dismissive-avoidant, fearful-avoidant.

Chapter 5. Nurture Over Nature?

- The age-old debate of nature versus nurture may never be settled definitively; rather, it should be said that they work together in all aspects of building one's identity.

- On the nurture side, social learning theory and the four variables (behavior potential, expectancy, reinforcement value, and psychological situation) give context to someone's identity. Regional and cultural differences also speak highly to the differences that a simple change in geography can cause in someone's identity.

- However, on the nature side, there has been shown to be a Neanderthal quotient measured in people who have very different personality traits from the rest of the population. The reality is that nature and nurture are intertwined too deeply and contribute equally to someone's adulthood identity.

Chapter 6. The Stories We Create

- Sometimes the best way to discover something about ourselves to is to ask seemingly innocent questions, then read between the lines. The way we answer these types of questions can be more honest and indicative than intentionally trying to figure out your personality and identity.
- The first way to do this is through the seven stories exercise, which implores you to find your seven greatest accomplishments and write the stories involved in those triumphs. What comes out in the story will tell you more about who you are and what you seek than trying to answer those questions alone.
- The second method to discover yourself is through Carl Jung's personality test, which consists of four questions: name a color, name an animal, name a body of water, and think about a white room. The

ensuing adjectives you use to describe each of those answers will tell you something specific about your personality that your psyche may not consciously have realized.

Chapter 7. Self-Awareness Questions

- Self-awareness is important, but not easily gained. That's why it's so highly valued.
- The best way to gain self-awareness is to ask about your behaviors and actions, not your intentions or thoughts. Your thoughts are too easily corrupted or otherwise simply not representative of what you actually feel. When you can analyze your behaviors and actions, you can then glean real information about yourself.

Chapter 8. Effecting Change

- Creating a change in your personality and identity is not as difficult as you may think. It is, however, perhaps more important than you might think. It can simultaneously make you feel happier and

more fulfilled while also avoiding malicious judgment from others.
- In fact, there have been 16 interrelated personality traits associated with well-being and happiness. It wouldn't do them justice to list them all out here, but it's a helpful guideline of what you can or should be changing.
- One of the ways to effectuate change is to change your environment and see the personality change as an adaptation. You can also focus on doing the change and not thinking about it, understanding motivations, setting clearer goals, and changing your self-narrative.

Chapter 9. Personality Potpourri

- We are all familiar with the concept of Type A and Type B personalities, but were you aware that there is certainly one type that will allow you to live longer and more happily? It's the type which lets you approach life from a less anxious lens: Type B.
- Transactional analysis is a theory of communication and roles. There are three

possible roles for us to take in any interaction, and which role we take depends on the other person: Parent, Adult, or Child. You may have noticed similar patterns in your own life where you felt you had to take charge (or the opposite) with specific people.

- Genders have different personalities, and though it begrudges me to say this, many of the differences you can already imagine due to intense gender stereotyping. Additionally, everything about a gender you think would be tied to an evolutionary basis also shows correlation.
- The Enneagram test is the final personality and identity test we cover in this book. It is composed of nine general types of personalities: reformer, helper, achiever, individualist, investigator, loyalist, enthusiast, challenger, and peacemaker.

www.ingramcontent.com/pod-product-compliance
Lightning Source LLC
Chambersburg PA
CBHW071159070526
44584CB00019B/2856